AWESOME GOD

NEIL T. ANDERSON
RICH MILLER

To Dustin,
    For your baptism, We
are happy to be able to share
this day with you!
                    Sept 17/99
        The Newsteads

HARVEST HOUSE PUBLISHERS
Eugene, Oregon 97402

Illustrated by Scott Angle.

Cover by Garborg Design Works, Minneapolis, Minnesota.

AWESOME GOD

Copyright © 1996 by Harvest House Publishers
Eugene, Oregon 97402

Library of Congress Cataloging-in-Publication Data
Anderson, Neil T., 1942–
    Awesome God / Neil T. Anderson and Rich Miller
        p. cm.
    Summary: Offers forty meditations to help teenagers learn to experience God's work in
        their lives.
    ISBN 1-56507-411-4
    1. Teenagers—Prayer-books and devotions—English. 2. God—Attributes—Prayer-
        books and devotions—English. [1. Prayer-books and devotions. 2. Christian life.]
        I. Miller, Rich, 1954– . II Title.
    BV4850.A53   1996
    242'.63—dc20   96-8503
                                                                        CIP
                                                                        AC

Printed in the United States of America.

            98   99   00   01   02   03   /BC/   10   9   8   7   6   5   4   3

Table of Contents

Our Awesome God 5

1. All Heaven Broke Loose 7
2. Don't Just Do Something, Stand There! 12
3. The Lonely Road 17
4. Father Knows Best 22
5. The Father You've Always Needed 28
6. In a Class by Himself 34
7. The High Way 40
8. The Way Up Is Down 46
9. East Never Meets West 51
10. Jehovah Jireh 56
11. When God Plays Hardball 61
12. Tornado! 66
13. I Couldn't Get Out of My Seat! 71
14. What's in a Name? 77
15. Patience Carries a Lot of Wait 82
16. Unclean! Unclean! 88
17. From Beginning to End and Beyond 93
18. Anybody Thirsty? 98
19. The God Who Heals 104
20. Join Up! Join In! 109
21. A Big, Big Heart 115
22. Go in Peace 121
23. The Devil's Worst Nightmare 126
24. It's a Small World After All 132
25. The God Who Serves 137

26. A Party Hearty in Heaven...................... 142
27. You Don't Mess Around with God............... 147
28. Thank God!.................................... 153
29. Count On It................................... 158
30. Accept or Except?............................. 164
31. Unquenchable Love 170
32. A Load Off My Mind........................... 175
33. A Lifetime Guarantee.......................... 180
34. It's a Spirit Thing 185
35. Out of This World............................. 191
36. Will the Real Jesus Please Stand Up? 197
37. Rock Solid.................................... 202
38. The Day Is Coming!............................ 208
39. The Buck Stops Here 213
40. The Final Victory 220

    Notes 225

OUR AWESOME GOD

When Michael Jordan takes off from the free-throw line and does a reverse one-handed jam, you explode out of your seat and cheer your head off. Awesome!

When your car emerges from the tunnel and there for the first time you see the snowcapped Colorado Rocky Mountains, you breathe a quiet "Whoa!" and just stare. Awesome!

When you watch the video taken by a storm chaser of an F-5 tornado spinning like a monstrous vacuum across the defenseless Texas countryside, you shake your head and pray a silent prayer of thanks for your safety and for mercy for those it leaves behind. Awesome!

Christian artist Rich Mullins' hit *Awesome God* has become a classic. It's fun to sing, sure, but there's more to its appeal than that. It reminds us that God is not a frail old gray-haired man in a rocking chair in the sky. He is the Lord! He does reign with wisdom, power and love. I'm afraid that, as the song warns, we have too quickly forgotten that our God *is* an awesome God.

We would like to do something to change all that, and that's why we wrote this book. We'd like to invite you on a journey—an adventure that will take us into the very throne room of God. A quest to rediscover the God who loves with an awesome love, radiates with an awesome holiness, and reigns with awesome wisdom, justice, and faithfulness.

Moses had an incredible opportunity (several times!) to spend 40 days on the mountain with God, up close and personal. Mountains are great, but you can meet with God wherever works for you. We do recommend, however, a quiet place where you can be alone.

Each chapter in this 40-day devotional will get you thinking about an aspect of God's character that you may not have thought much about before. You will then have the chance to respond to what you've read. Most days you will find *THE LIE TO REJECT* and *THE TRUTH TO ACCEPT*. We encourage you to say these out loud, thinking about what you're reading. If you have believed lies about God, this exercise will help you choose the truth instead.

Following that exercise, there is the *PRAYER FOR TODAY*. It's a great chance to express back to God thoughts and feelings related to that day's message.

It's important to let God speak to you directly through His Word, so we have included two chances to do just that. *READ ALL ABOUT IT* provides a chapter of Scripture that relates to that day's topic. *GOING DEEPER WITH GOD* takes you through four books of the Bible (Matthew, 1 Peter, Philippians, and 2 Peter), one chapter a day.

Don't feel under the pile with each day's reading and exercises. Look at them as opportunities to spend time with God. You can take as much or as little time each day as you wish.

The key is consistency. Doing something, even if it's just a little bit each day, is best. If you're like us, you will find that the time spent in the presence of God is so awesome that the minutes go by really fast. And you may just find yourself wanting to hang out with God longer than you first thought!

God is in a class by Himself. He really is an *Awesome God*. Why not take a 40-day journey with us and see for yourself? The view is awesome!

ALL HEAVEN BROKE LOOSE

When all the people saw it, they fell on their faces; and they said, "The LORD, He is God; the LORD, He is God" (1 Kings 18:39).

The people had nothing. Their meager food supply barely kept them from starvation. There was no water for their thirsty bodies. What's worse, there was no hope for their thirsty souls. They were walking skeletons in an African refugee camp.

Then the messengers came, not armed with weapons, but with a movie screen, a projector and a film on the life of Jesus. God had heard the cries of the people and was bringing them a message of hope.

But the cruel hater of all hope, Satan, was not going to give up easily. As the film team set up, they "heard witch doctors chanting and saw them throwing bones on the ground in satanic rituals. With howling and incantations, the witch doctors began calling up spirits of their ancestors. An eerie and foreboding pall seemed to fall over the camp."[1]

So the team prayed. For three hours they stood their ground against the enemy's attacks, pleading with God to tear down the devil's strongholds and set the refugees free. And the witch doctors stopped. They were up against a power they had never known before—the power of an awesome God.

7

About a thousand men, women, and children huddled around the screen, watching the Gospel of Luke unfold before them. When the crucifixion of Jesus was shown in the movie, all heaven broke loose. Here is the eyewitness account as told in Paul Eshleman's book *The Touch of Jesus:*

> They ignored all the ropes, and huge clouds of dust filled the air as people watching from both sides of the screen rushed to the front.
>
> Rivers of tears poured down dirty cheeks. Young men, old men, and women beat their breasts and cried out; "Oh, God! Oh, God!"... Everywhere people were confessing their sins.... These people were in the presence of a holy God, and they were overwhelmed....
>
> They saw the burial of Christ, and then—the resurrection. The interpreter explained to the crowd, "Jesus died to make the payment for our sins. But death could not hold Him." And with that, he pointed to the screen and shouted with uncontainable joy, "And there He is! He was raised from the dead!"
>
> The crowd exploded as if a dam had burst. Everyone began cheering and dancing and hugging one another and jumping up and down.[2]

The result? One thousand hopeless people found Hope, the Lord Jesus Christ. They all wanted to accept Him as Savior and Lord! Next Sunday, 500 new believers showed up at a church building made to hold 40![3]

In the days of King Ahab of Israel there was also a famine in the land. It had not rained for 42 months. The people were confused. They weren't sure who to worship anymore. And so Elijah, the John Wayne of Old Testament prophets, offered a challenge to the false prophets of Baal (a demon masquerading as a fertility god): a face-to-face showdown on Mount Carmel.

Elijah wanted to make sure the event was a sellout, so he got in the face of the people and shouted:

> "How long will you hesitate between two opinions? If the Lord is God, follow Him; but if Baal, follow him." But the people did not answer him a word" (1 Kings 18:21).

The stage was set. The false prophets were instructed to make an altar and put an ox on it. Then they would call on Baal to send fire from heaven and burn it up. The crowd watched in anticipation.

All morning and afternoon they danced and screamed and cut themselves, trying to get Baal to answer them. Nothing. Elijah couldn't resist the urge to get in a little dig. "Hey, maybe he's asleep or away on vacation or just thinking!" he shouted. I'm sure the audience was enjoying the show.

When evening came, it was Elijah's turn. To add to the drama of the moment, he poured a ton of water over the sacrifice and soaked it thoroughly. Then he prayed a simple prayer to God. No hype. No fanfare. No glitz. Just faith. And God answered:

> Then fire of the LORD fell, and consumed the burnt offering and the wood and the stones and the dust, and licked up the water that was in the trench. And when all the people saw it, they fell on their faces; and they said, "The LORD, He is God; the LORD, He is God" (1 Kings 18:38,39).

There you have it. Two instances, one modern-day and one ancient, when God had mercy on a starving, confused, hopeless group of people. He showed His awesome power because He wanted them to know beyond a shadow of a doubt that the LORD is God.

Maybe you're saying to yourself, "Well, that's great for them. But what about me? I've never seen God's power at work like that."

Really?

On the day you opened your heart to heaven through Jesus Christ, the old you went up in smoke. Like a flash of lightning, all the dry dust and hard stone of your soul was blasted away. In the twinkling of an eye you became a new creation in Christ.

God swept away your darkness and exploded light into the deepest shadows of your life. And from the depths of your soul you cried out for mercy, saying, "The LORD, He is God; the LORD, He is God."

That all may have happened at such an early age that you don't remember it. Maybe you were too young to know what hit you. Or maybe it happened more recently. You knew something good occurred at that time, but in your more reflective moments you're saying, "Well, that was nice, but what have You done for me lately, God?"

Know one thing for sure: *The awesome God still lives in you.* He has set up His throne in your heart. Will you let Him reign?

If you bow your heart before Christ the King, we'll assure you of this: Although we don't know exactly what it will look like in your life, we know that you'll see all heaven break loose in you and through you.

The Lie to Reject

I reject the lie that God works powerfully in and through

*other people's lives, but He won't do that for me. I refuse
to accept a humdrum, drab, and confused life of doubt and
unbelief.*

THE TRUTH TO ACCEPT

*I accept the truth that the God who worked in others wants
to work in me as well. I anticipate with faith the powerful
moving of my awesome God in my life today.*

PRAYER FOR TODAY

*Dear Lord, forgive me for my unbelief. I have many times
doubted Your willingness to work in my life in a powerful way. I thank You for Elijah's example of bold faith,
trusting You even when outnumbered. Sometimes I feel
overwhelmed by the sin around me, but I know that You
are awesome and that when You are on my side, together
we can see all heaven break loose. Show me today what to
believe You for in my own life and in the lives of those
around me. In Jesus' name. Amen.*

READ ALL ABOUT IT

1 Kings 18

GOING DEEPER WITH GOD

Matthew 1

Don't Just Do Something, Stand There!

Thus the Lord God, the Holy One of Israel, has said: "In repentance and rest you shall be saved, In quietness and trust is your strength" (Isaiah 30:15).

Fast food. Fast lanes. Fast cars. Fast cash. Fast action. No doubt about it, we live in a fast-paced world. Even though most of us sort of ooze out of bed in the morning, we soon kick into high gear. Rocketing through breakfast, we race out the door to make it to school on time. Our minds filled with ricocheting thoughts, we fly through a day jam-packed with classes, extracurricular activities, meals, homework, friends, phone calls, TV, computer chat rooms, video games, ad exhaustium.

And then we collapse into bed at night (or early morning!) listening to music that sends a fresh dose of adrenaline exploding through our bodies.

It seems like we never really have time to *unwind*. We just *rewind*.

With our brains on overload, is it any wonder we sometimes feel like our emotions have short-circuited and we're just running on fumes?

Before we all crash and burn in a ditch somewhere along the information superhighway, maybe we need to stop, look, and listen . . . for just a second, anyway.

That's what Elijah, that powerful prophet of God, had to do. He had just come off the incredible experience we talked about in yesterday's devotional, defeating the 850 false prophets by the power of Almighty God.

Then Elijah prayed seven times for rain, and God answered his prayer with a gully-washer that ended a 3 ½ year drought!

Later that same day, with the hand of the Lord on him, that man of God outran the king's chariot from Mount Carmel to Jezreel—about the distance of a marathon!

What an incredible day of experiencing the awesomeness of God! Surely Elijah was on a spiritual high, bursting with faith, hope, and love, right? Wrong! He actually found himself spiraling into a black hole of doubt, fear, and self-pity. Elijah was depressed.

What happened? Wicked Queen Jezebel happened. She had put out a contract on Elijah's life and swore that within 24 hours that prophet would meet the same fate as the 850 false prophets—death. And so Elijah ran for his life.

Exhausted, Elijah pleaded with God to let him die. Instead, God let him entertain himself in his one-man pity party for over 40 days, graciously providing food and water to sustain him on the way.

Finally Elijah ended up in a cave on a mountain, still whining for God to grant him a one-way ticket off the planet. But God had other plans for His servant. He made an offer Elijah could not refuse: He told him to stop, look, and listen. Let's pick up the story in 1 Kings 19:11-13:

> So He said, "Go forth, and stand on the mountain before the Lord." And behold, the Lord was passing by! And a great and strong wind was rending the mountains and breaking in pieces the rocks before

the Lord; but the Lord was not in the wind. And
after the wind an earthquake, but the Lord was not
in the earthquake. And after the earthquake a fire,
but the Lord was not in the fire; and after the fire a
sound of a gentle blowing. And it came about when
Elijah heard it, that he wrapped his face in his mantle,
and went out and stood in the entrance of the cave.
And behold, a voice came to him, and said, "What
are you doing here, Elijah?"

A wind strong enough to shatter rock? An earthquake?
A fire on the mountain? Surely God would speak through
those things! And sometimes He does, but not this time. This
time he spoke in a whisper like the sound of a gentle evening
breeze through the pines. A still, small voice. A quiet, soothing
rustling that Elijah had not heard for a while.

He had been too busy running to listen. Thrilled by victory, driven by fear, exhausted from travel, he had forgotten
how to hear from God.

Have you by any chance forgotten, too?

You see, the same God who spoke to Elijah wants to
speak to you today. He is here and He indeed is not silent.
The God who spoke and billions of galaxies instantly were
hurled into space wants to speak to *you*. The God who knows
the name of each one of the stars, as well as the number of
hairs on your head, wants to speak to *you*.

He is the God who created you, who calls you by name,
and who knows you like a book—because He is the Author.

You might say that He is the *intimate infinite.*

He is here and He is still speaking . . . through His creation, His Word, His people, His Spirit, and best of all,
through His Son.

Jesus' sheep listen to His voice, and He knows them and they follow Him. But His voice is quiet. The busy, preoccupied, hurried, and worried teenager will not hear Him.

He wants to speak with you today—to lead, to guide, to protect, to empower, to love. Are you listening?

Will you follow the quiet, unseen, unhurried Shepherd and Guardian of your soul? The gentle, humble Jesus invites you to join Him on a journey of faith.

It is a walk on the path of truth. It is an adventure on the road of freedom.

So why not take a deep breath and let it out slowly. That's it. Do it again. Let it be a sigh of relief for you.

Recognize that "in repentance and rest you shall be saved." *Repentance* is changing your mind and choosing to go God's way instead of your own. *Rest* is ceasing from your labors and allowing God to strengthen you to do His. Then you will be saved from being worn out, wiped out, stressed out, and burned out!

Know today that "in quietness and trust is your strength." Not in endless noise, ceaseless activity, and frenzied busyness. In quietness and trust.

The world says, "Don't just stand there, do something!" But in today's fast-paced world, perhaps God is saying to you, "Don't just do something, stand there!"

THE LIE TO REJECT

I reject the lie of the world that says I cannot be happy

unless I keep moving. I refuse to accept the lie that spending quiet time with God is dull, boring, and unprofitable.

THE TRUTH TO ACCEPT

I accept the truth that I desperately need to spend quiet and peaceful time with my heavenly Father. I choose to believe the truth that I will find strength through quiet trust in God.

PRAYER FOR TODAY

Dear Lord, please forgive me for getting so caught up and wrapped up in the things of life that I have neglected time with You. You are my life, and I want to get to know You as the awesome God You are. I thank You that You love me and want to lead me into truth that will set me free today. I want to be free from worry, hurry, fear, doubt, and depression. I choose to stop, look, and listen for Your still, small voice. Please reveal Yourself to me. In Jesus' name I pray. Amen.

READ ALL ABOUT IT

1 Kings 19

GOING DEEPER WITH GOD

Matthew 2

THE LONELY ROAD

"Blessed be the Lord, who daily bears our burden, the God who is our salvation" (Psalm 68:19).

It was Christmastime. " 'Tis the season to be jolly" and all that. But to be honest with you, I was miserable. It was the first time I had been away from home for Christmas, and with every mile of road I traveled, I felt the emptiness grow.

I was driving alone from Ohio to California to join a youth ministry in Southern California. You might be thinking, "Wow! Southern California—the sun, the sand, the surf. What a blast!" But I was thinking, "Oh no, the land of the fruits, the nuts, and the flakes. The smog capital of the world."

My first day driving west was awful. I needed wind-shield wipers for my eyes, I was crying so hard. Feeling like my heart was being ripped out of the Midwestern soil I had grown to love, I grieved for the friends I was leaving behind. Have you ever broken up with a steady boyfriend or girl-friend? That's what it felt like. Not fun at all.

On Christmas Eve I made it into Oklahoma to stay with the family of one of my new California co-workers. She was having a merry Christmas with her folks, but I couldn't wait to get out of the house. Each joyful laugh from that family seemed to twist the knife of loneliness deeper into my heart.

I declined their invitation to spend Christmas Day with them, waved a quick goodbye, and hit the road early

Christmas morning. I couldn't bear the thought of watching them open presents! Somewhere in west Texas late that Christmas afternoon I had it out with the Lord.

"Lord, I've prayed for days now that You would make Your presence known to me and fill the awful emptiness inside me. But all I've felt is grief. I don't even have any more tears to cry. Don't You care?"

But there was only silence.

Early Christmas night I rolled into a motel somewhere in eastern New Mexico, tired and sad. I flopped down on my bed and dialed my parents' house back in Pennsylvania. All the telephone circuits were busy, and they remained that way all night long.

I had never felt so alone in my life.

Our friend, Elijah, experienced intense loneliness too. In running from Jezebel, he complained to the Lord:

> I have been very zealous for the Lord God Almighty. The Israelites have rejected your covenant, broken down your altars, and put your prophets to death with the sword. I am the only one left, and now they are trying to kill me too" (1 Kings 19:14 NIV).

God responded by giving the prophet a job to do. Then he calmed his fears by telling him that he was not alone at all:

> "Yet I will leave 7,000 in Israel, all the knees that have not bowed to Baal and every mouth that has not kissed him" (1 Kings 19:18).

Elijah wasn't alone, and neither are you. God is able to meet the deepest needs of your soul. At times He'll use other people, and at times He'll do it Himself. Scripture says, "Draw near to God and He will draw near to you" (James 4:8). That is a promise you can bank on.

A year or so earlier I had been very alone on a Saturday night and decided to see if God could fill the empty places in my soul. After two hours in the Word and prayer, I rose to my feet feeling deeply satisfied.

God at that time had shown me what David meant when he wrote, "My soul is satisfied as with marrow and fatness, and my mouth offers praises with joyful lips" (Psalm 63:5). Could He do it again? Would He?

In my motel room I could have tried to drown out my sorrow by flipping on the tube, but I didn't. I chose to talk to God and see what He might have to say to me.

After listening to all my fussing and fuming, the Lord finally spoke to me through Psalms 31 and 68. He had been trying to get through to me for days with these portions of Scripture, but I had been grieving too hard to hear Him. Now I was just numb.

My eyes turned once again to Psalm 31:9 and I honestly prayed, "Be gracious to me, O LORD, for I am in distress; my eye is wasted away from grief, my soul and my body also."

I kept on reading, and verses 14 and 15 hit me like a ton of bricks:

> But I trust in you, O LORD; I say, "You are my God."
> My times are in your hands (Psalm 31:14,15 NIV).

And then Psalm 68:19:

> Blessed be the Lord, who daily bears our burden,
> the God who is our salvation.

I had known in my head before that He would never leave me nor forsake me (Hebrews 13:5), but then I knew it in my heart. Again.

My exodus from the Midwest to a land filled with strange things and strange people in California was all part of God's plan. I learned that on earth the goodbye's are as much God's will as the hello's. Until we get to heaven, that is. Heaven is going to be one long hello and no more goodbye's.

My mind went back to something I had heard preacher Ron Dunn say once before: *You'll never know God is all you need until He's all you've got.*

I was beginning to understand what he meant.

I realized at that moment that my times *were* in God's hands, and that He was bearing my burden with me. Actually, He had been doing so from the moment I had started my journey.

Then suddenly it dawned on me: Hey, this is *Christmas!* And Christmas isn't really Christmas trees and presents and being home, although all those things are nice. Christmas is *Jesus,* and He spent the first one in accommodations a lot less glamorous than the motel room I was in!

My spirits began to lift, and I actually found myself beginning to look forward to the adventure that lay ahead of me in California.

But for now I felt too much joy to sit in my room, so I went down to the lobby and talked with the man at the desk. After all, he was away from his home and family too. And I wanted to introduce him to the family that had come with me on my trip: my brother, Jesus, whose birthday we were celebrating, and my Father, God, who was bearing my burden with me.

The Lie to Reject

I reject the lie that I am alone. I refuse to believe my feelings when they tell me God has deserted me. I will not allow tough circumstances to convince me that the Lord has abandoned me.

THE TRUTH TO ACCEPT

I accept the truth that the God who daily bears my burdens will never leave me nor forsake me. I choose to believe that He will always be there for me and that He holds my life and times in His loving hand.

PRAYER FOR TODAY

Dear Father, this really is a walk by faith, isn't it? I'm so used to living by what my feelings tell me, but now I'm starting to see that this is wrong. Thank You that You are my unseen companion wherever I go and wherever I am. During those times when You wisely withhold from me a sense of Your presence, help me not to panic but to cling to You by faith. Thank You that Your right hand will always uphold me. I pray in the name of Jesus, who promised to be with me even to the end of the age. Amen.

READ ALL ABOUT IT

Psalm 31

GOING DEEPER WITH GOD

Matthew 3

DAY FOUR

FATHER KNOWS BEST

When you are praying, do not use meaningless repetition, as the Gentiles do, for they suppose that they will be heard for their many words. Therefore do not be like them, for your Father knows what you need, before you ask Him" (Matthew 6:7,8).

It was a golden late fall afternoon in northern Georgia. The air was cool and brisk, without a hint of the drippy humidity that mildews the mind during summer in the South.

Standing in the sun, I felt the rays gently toast the chill away from my arms and face. It was a day filled with a thousand reasons to give thanks to God, the most obvious being that it was Thanksgiving!

Enjoying the day and the conversation around me, I happened to overhear a little girl talking to a group of adults. She was upset. As I tuned in closer to her words, I found out she had lost her ring while playing in the leaves down the street. It was a precious ring to her, one that had been passed down to her from her mom.

Sensing a nudge inside from the Lord, I went over and asked if I could help her find it. She said, "Sure," so she, her friend, and I started walking down the street to the scene of the "crime."

I thought it was a good idea to pray, and so I did out loud: *Lord, please help us find this ring, because You know where it is and we sure don't. In Jesus' name. Amen.*

A pretty basic, no-frills kind of prayer, I'll admit, but I was feeling confident. Yes, sir, "Ace Miller, Ring Detective" to the rescue!

When we got to the place where she had lost the ring, I groaned. The dead leaves on the ground were at least a foot thick. This was not going to be easy.

I came up with a strategy to try to simplify things. I had her stand where she had been when the ring fell off and demonstrate what she had been doing. She had been trying to catch falling leaves, and one time while she was reaching up the ring had flown off her finger.

So, logical person that I am, I marked out a rectangular area in front of and behind her where I figured the ring would have landed. And so we went to work. Leaf by leaf we started clearing the area, looking for the missing ring.

Ten minutes went by, then 15. Still no ring. I prayed again silently, *Lord, please help us find this ring. It means a lot to this little girl.*

Twenty minutes went by, then 25, but still no ring. To be honest with you, I began to doubt that God was going to come through. Angrily I prayed, *C'mon, Lord! Help us find it! Don't You care about this little girl's ring? She needs to know that You care about the things that are important to her! In Jesus' name. Amen.*

Looking back, the way I prayed must have been a bit amusing to God. I was honest, which is always good, but I was really doing more yelling than praying. And then, just to make it "kosher," I added "In Jesus' name. Amen" at the end. I'm sure glad God is patient!

After about a half-hour of searching we had cleared every leaf out of the target area. I was at the end of my wits when suddenly a car pulled up along the curb.

An old man, and I mean a *very* old man, stopped the car, rolled down the window, leaned over, and asked in a classic Southern drawl, "Y'all lose somethin'?"

At that moment every sarcastic bone in my body wanted to reply, "No, our family always spends Thanksgiving afternoon groveling around in dried leaves!" Instead I said without looking up, "Yeah, she lost her ring."

"Mind if I help?" he continued.

I couldn't believe it. Silently I yelled at God again, *Oh, thank You, Lord! Is this the best You can do? You send along a guy so old he can barely see to drive. He's got one foot in the grave and another on a banana peel.*

Fortunately I didn't say any of that. Instead I answered, "Sure, why not?"

And then the Lord did one of those "God things" that makes you sit down and shut up.

The man got out of his car, walked around to his trunk, opened it up, and pulled out a metal detector.

Inside I was saying, "Oh Lord, I'm so sorry."

After five minutes of looking, the metal detector's beeper went off and there was the ring. It was about two inches outside my "inspired" target area, by the way.

The little girl, who had started back to the house to use the bathroom, came running back as we shouted and held up the ring. Overjoyed, she put it on her finger and raced home and told everybody the great thing that *God* had done for her.

Later on, after I returned home, I was thinking about the whole incident. I was kind of congratulating God for what He had done. *Y'know, Lord, You're all right. You really came through in the clutch. That little girl needed to know that You care.*

The impression on my mind was immediate and unmistakable. I knew it was the Lord. *No, Rich,* you *needed to know that I care.*

And so I did.

Maybe today *you* need to know, too.

Jesus taught us to pray in a different way than non-Christians do. The pagans try to impress God with their seriousness by repeating their prayers over and over again. They act as if God doesn't really care or that He's too busy to listen, so they have to bug Him to death until He finally gives in.

But our God is not like that. He is our Father, and He knows what we need even before we ask Him.

So why ask? *Because He wants us to learn to depend on Him.* God doesn't need our prayers to inform Him of what's going on in our lives, because He already knows. We need to humble ourselves before the One who alone can meet those needs. And that One is not a mean, cruel, and uncaring God; He is our Father. Jesus put it this way in Matthew 7:7-11:

> Ask, and it shall be given to you; seek, and you shall find; knock, and it shall be opened to you. For everyone who asks receives, and he who seeks finds, and to him who knocks it shall be opened. Or what man is there among you, when his son shall ask him for a loaf, will give him a stone? Or if he shall ask for a fish, he will not give him a snake, will he? If you then, being evil, know how to give good gifts

to your children, how much more shall your Father
who is in heaven give what is good to those who
ask Him!

Do you need help? Go ahead and ask God. You will
receive. Do you need wisdom? Go ahead and seek God. You
will find. Do you need a door to be opened for your life and
ministry? Go ahead and knock. It will be opened for you.

Whatever your needs, you can trust God today. Why?
Because Father knows best.

The Lie to Reject

*I reject the lie that God doesn't care about my needs or
that He's too busy to bother with me. I refuse to believe
the devil's lies that I must fend for myself.*

The Truth to Accept

*I accept the truth that my Father knows what I need before
I ask Him and that He is a generous God who delights in
answering prayer. I choose to believe that He will provide,
even if that provision does not come right away.*

Prayer for Today

*Dear Lord, You are my Father. I thank You that You hear
my prayers the first time I pray them. I'm so glad that You
love me and are always listening to me. You are the all-wise
God who knows what I need and when I need it. Thank
You for the times You say no because You see that what I
am asking for is not good for me. Thank You for the times
You say "wait" because you know I'm not yet ready. I*

choose to completely trust You today to take care of me. You are the perfect Father. I pray all this in the name of the Son You gave to die for me. Amen.

Read All About It

Psalm 145

Going Deeper with God

Matthew 4

The Father You've Always Needed

You have not received a spirit of slavery leading to fear again, but you have received a spirit of adoption as sons by which we cry out, "Abba! Father!" The Spirit Himself bears witness with our spirit that we are children of God (Romans 8:15,16).

I felt pretty important. I was about to have a personal counseling session with a ten-year veteran NFL football player. All expenses paid...by him!

On his day off, we sat down across the table in my hotel room and prepared to go through *The Steps to Freedom in Christ*. It would take over four hours to complete.

Money was no object for this man, but I would not have traded places in life with him for one minute. He had serious family problems on top of his own spiritual struggles. A lot of it seemed to stem from his inability to maintain a consistent relationship of love and trust with God the Father.

There was no doubt in my mind that he had trusted Jesus Christ as his Savior, but consistently yielding to Him as Lord was another matter altogether.

I probed a bit as I tried to figure out why he viewed God as distant from him and disinterested in his life. There didn't seem to be any major abuse or neglect in his past, though his dad seemed like he was gone an awful lot.

Then a thought came to me, so I decided to check it out.

"You know, I've talked to a number of athletes in my life who were really hurt because their parents never came to their games."

The man looked at me like I had shot him with a gun. "That's it," he replied, shaking. "From the time I was in junior high, through high school and college, and now ten years in the pro's, my parents have never come to one of my games."

I was shocked, and truly felt sorry for the guy. But I was not prepared for what happened next.

All 240 pounds of solid muscle started quivering as he began to sob. He was crying out 20 years of pain, and I couldn't help but cry with him.

"Y'know, Rich," he said, "Every time I play in a game, I'm so afraid I'll mess up. Even if I catch ten passes in a row, I'm scared to death I'll drop the eleventh."

Realizing what was going on, I responded quietly, "You've tried all your life to play the perfect game, hoping you'd finally be good enough that your parents would come and watch you play.

"And you've assumed that your heavenly Father was just like your earthly dad—distant and disinterested. But God your Father has never missed one of your games. He is the Father you have always needed and wanted."

That did it. The floodgates of tears burst open and he ran into the bathroom to get more tissues. But these were tears that had to be shed so this man could be free to cry out, "Abba! [Daddy!] Father!" to God.

Next Sunday I happened to be watching the day's NFL highlights, and to my delight, guess who caught a touchdown pass?

I called him up to congratulate him and what he said told me he had "got it." He was free.

He said, "Rich, this was the first time in my entire life that I really enjoyed playing a football game! The anxiety is gone."

Like this man, perhaps you've believed some lies about your heavenly Father, and that has distorted your view of Him. Maybe you've struggled with your ability to trust Him, not sure He will be there for you.

The following exercise is designed to help break down any strongholds of wrong thinking that you may have about your heavenly Father. In the left column are some phrases describing how you might view God. They are all lies. In the right-hand column is the truth.

Read both lists out loud, moving down the columns left to right, left to right, and so on. Start each statement on the left with the words "I reject the lie that my Father God is . . . " Begin each statement on the right with the words "I joyfully accept the truth that my Father God is . . . "

No matter how hard it is to make it through this exercise, hang in there and don't give up until you've finished it. It could have a profound effect on your life and help make the rest of this devotional far more meaningful to you. It is the *truth* that sets you free (John 8:32).

I reject the lie that my Father God is...

1. distant and disinterested

2. insensitive and uncaring

3. stern and demanding

4. passive and cold

5. absent or too busy for me

6. never satisfied with what I do, impatient, or angry

7. mean, cruel, or abusive

8. trying to take all the fun out of life

9. controlling or manipulative

10. nit-picking or exacting

I joyfully accept the truth that my Father God is...

1. intimate and involved

2. kind and compassionate

3. accepting and filled with joyful love

4. warm and affectionate

5. always with me and eager to spend time with me

6. patient, slow to anger, and pleased with me in Christ

7. loving, gentle, and protective of me

8. trustworthy and desiring to give me a full life. His will is good, perfect, and acceptable for me.

9. full of grace and mercy, and giving me the freedom to fail

10. smiling as He thinks of me and pleased with me as His growing child

I am the apple of His eye!

A young lady who had grown to hate her angry, controlling dad struggled with intimacy with God. After reading through a list similar to this, she began praying with the words "Our heavenly Father..." Then she stopped, looked up at me, and smiled.

"I've prayed prayers to my heavenly Father all my life, because you're supposed to pray 'Our Father who art in heaven...' But this time, just now when I prayed, was the first time I *felt* something."

What was happening?

Like many Christians, this young lady had all the right answers. If you had asked her, "Does God loves you?" she would have answered, "Of course." If you had then asked her, "How do you know God loves you?" she would have replied without batting an eyelash, "Because Christ died for me."

All these answers would have been exactly right, but they were all in her head, not in her heart. When she read through the list, rejecting the lies and choosing the truth about God, the wall between her head and heart came tumbling down.

Maybe you've struggled with developing a close friendship with God. Maybe you've had a barrier between your head and heart as well. Or maybe you've felt like that wall was between you and God.

Don't believe the devil's slanderous lies. Choose the truth. God indeed is the Father you have always needed and wanted.

Prayer for Today

Dear Father, I know I have believed things that were not true about You. At times I have listened to the devil's slan-

derous attacks on Your good character. I have even been angry with You when You did not act how and when I thought You should have. Thank You for forgiving me for my lack of love and faith. More than anything else I want to know You as You truly are and to love You with all my heart, soul, mind, and strength. Please continue revealing Your sweet Self to me, for I know that worshiping You is what I was created to do. I look forward to developing a deeper intimacy with You than I ever thought possible. And it is through Your Son, Jesus, that I pray. Amen.

Read All About It

Romans 8

Going Deeper with God

Matthew 5

Day Six

In a Class by Himself

Who among the gods is like you, O LORD? Who is like you—majestic in holiness, awesome in glory, working wonders? (Exodus 15:11 NIV).

Millions of people every year stay glued to the tube on a Sunday in late January. "Super Sunday," it's called, the day the NFL crowns its annual champion in the Super Bowl. Baseball has its heyday every October, when the "Fall Classic," the World Series, unfolds its drama before the riveted attention of millions. The Masters Golf Tournament in Augusta, Georgia, swings into play each azalea-blossoming spring. The U.S. Open Tennis Tournament cooks in the sweltering heat of a New York City summer. March heralds the arrival of the NCAA basketball tournament, nicknamed "March Madness." The action-packed Stanley Cup and NBA playoffs soon follow.

Every year, each sport seeks to determine which team or individual is "number one." And when that team or individual successfully defends their crown year after year, people start comparing them to champions of old, wondering who is the all-time greatest.

Is four-time Cy Young award-winning pitcher Greg Maddux the best ever? Will any college basketball team ever match the dynasty of the UCLA teams under legendary coach John Wooden? Who is number one in women's tennis—Steffi Graf, Monica Seles, or someone else?

But beyond all the glory, glamour, and glitz of professional sports and stars is one event that surpasses them all—an event that even the pro's drool to be a part of, an event that is seen on TV by literally billions of people every four years: the Olympics.

As I write this, the world awaits the "Great Gold Rush of 96," the Summer Olympics in Atlanta. As you read this, the last exhausted marathoner will have braved the awful heat and humidity of a Georgia summer afternoon and the grandeur of the closing ceremonies will be history.

As happens in any athletic contest, most Olympians will fail to reach the goal they strove for and sweated a lifetime to attain: a medal. Some will lose by fractions of a second. Others will be tragically sidelined by illness or injury. Most will lose out to better-trained, better-talented, and better-conditioned athletes.

Then there are the winners—the few, the proud, the gold medalists. Beating personal bests and sometimes smashing world records, they stand proudly on the platform basking in the glory of victory.

At that moment and until the next world-class competition, that triumphant athlete can honestly be called "the best in the world."

What if you had the chance to have a private dinner with the Olympic champion soccer team, or the gold medal winner in boxing, or the decathlon—would you be excited about having that honor? Wouldn't you tell everyone who would listen all about it? Of course you would. Anybody would.

The Bible says that we have the opportunity to spend time with the Most High God, Jesus Christ. Jesus gives this invitation to each of us: "Here I am! I stand at the door and knock. If anyone hears my voice and opens the door, I will come in and eat with him, and he with me" (Revelation 3:20 NIV).

You might be tempted to think, "So what? What's the big deal about that? Jesus isn't exactly a star athlete or anything."

True, Jesus never won an Olympic gold medal, but Colossians 1:17 says of Him, "He is before all things, and in Him all things hold together." *All things.* That includes you and me and the entire universe. Jesus holds it all together. Pretty impressive, I'd say. Still not convinced that Jesus would have anything interesting to talk about? Just listen to this true story of an awesome display of God's power.

The Israelites were in the process of cleaning up the Promised Land by wiping out all the wicked people who lived there. General Joshua was leading a military campaign against five kings and their armies, but he had a problem. It was getting dark and he needed more time to mop up the operation. So he prayed that God would stop the sun.

No problem for God. Listen to the story:

> And the sun stopped in the middle of the sky, and did not hasten to go down for about a whole day. And there was no day like that before it or after it, when the LORD listened to the voice of a man; for the LORD fought for Israel (Joshua 10:13,14).

Can you imagine the sheer terror and confusion among people all over the planet, wondering what in the world was going on? On the other side of the earth people woke up in the morning, but it was still night. At high noon it was still pitch black. They must have thought it was the end of the world!

But it was no big deal for God. He keeps the earth spinning like a top anyway. All He probably did was stick out

His "little finger" and stop it for 24 hours. That made it appear like the sun was standing still.

What incredible power! What an awesome display of God's glory! And He did it in response to Joshua's prayer! In the words of Pastor E.V. Hill, "If that don't ring your bell, your clapper's busted!"

Is it any wonder that the Bible frequently asks questions like:

> Who among the gods is like you, O Lord?

Psalm 89:6-8 NIV says:

> Who in the skies above can compare with the Lord? Who is like the Lord among the heavenly beings? In the council of the holy ones God is greatly feared; he is more awesome than all who surround him. O Lord God Almighty, who is like you?

Psalm 113:4-6 NIV echoes the same theme:

> The Lord is exalted over all the nations, his glory above the heavens. Who is like the Lord our God, the One who sits enthroned on high, who stoops down to look on the heavens and the earth?

God Himself proclaims that no one is His equal in Isaiah 40:25,26:

> "To whom then will you liken Me that I should be his equal?" says the Holy One. Lift up your eyes on high and see who has created these stars, the One who leads forth their host by number, He calls them all by name; because of the greatness of His might and the strength of His power not one of them is missing.

When God's Word or God Himself asks the question "Who is like the Lord?" the obvious answer is "Absolutely no one!" There is no one in heaven or earth like Him. There is no one greater; there is no one even close.

And this incredibly awesome God has invited us to have a meal with Him—that is, to have a time of close, intimate fellowship. Now that's something to get excited about! Will you accept Jesus' invitation to spend time and get to know Him? I can tell you from experience that there's no friend like Him. He is truly in a class by Himself!

THE LIE TO REJECT

I reject the habit of taking God for granted and failing to see my relationship with Him as an incredible privilege and invitation to spend time with the Lord of all.

THE TRUTH TO ACCEPT

I accept the truth that there is no one like God and that in His presence is the fullness of joy. I will consider it the greatest thing in my life to be able to spend time with Him.

PRAYER FOR TODAY

Dear Father, there is no one like You, either in heaven or on earth. You showed me a glimpse of Your awesomeness by easily stopping the sun from going down for a whole day. How could I ever take You for granted or yawn at the thought of spending time with You? Please forgive me for being so blind to the wonderful invitation to have fellowship with Jesus, the King of all kings and Lord of all lords. Would You put a yearning in my heart to be with You that would surpass any other relationship in my life by far? When I think that one day I will actually see You face-to-face, I get excited. Until that day please help me experience a genuine excitement about meeting with You through prayer and Your Word. In Your name, Jesus. Amen.

READ ALL ABOUT IT
Joshua 10

GOING DEEPER WITH GOD
Matthew 6

THE HIGH WAY

Pray, then, in this way: "Our Father who art in heaven, hallowed be Thy name" (Matthew 6:9).

Apollo 13 is a great movie. The story depicts the dramatic voyage of a lunar-landing mission gone haywire. Because of terrible damage to the spacecraft, there is no way they can make it to the moon. The question is, will they make it back to earth?

The suspense builds as they realize that time is not on their side. The carbon dioxide level in the cabin is rising to a dangerous level and one of the crew is seriously ill. Then to make matters worse the men are basically on their own to navigate through the earth's atmosphere. Their high-tech guidance equipment is useless.

Rocketing through space toward earth at thousands of miles per hour, they must enter the atmosphere at precisely the right angle. If the angle is wrong they will either burn up like a shooting star or skip off Earth's atmosphere back into space like a rock skimming off a pond.

The powerful magnetic pull of Earth's gravity would either draw them home to safety or send them to their deaths. One way or the other they had an appointment with planet Earth that could not be stopped and would not be easy.

"So what's the point?" you may be asking. That's a good question. After all, you didn't pick up today's devotional to read a movie review.

In the beginning of what we call "The Lord's Prayer," Jesus teaches us how to address God: *Our Father who art in heaven, hallowed be Thy name.*

Hallowed? Like Halloween? Hardly, although the root words are the same. *Hallowed* basically means *holy.* God is holy, and when we come to Him in prayer we are to realize that we are in the presence of the Holy One.

Now here's the tie-in to our *Apollo 13* illustration: *God's love draws us toward Him with a power as magnetic as the earth's gravity pull on that spacecraft.* And God is "not wishing for any to perish but for all to come to repentance" (2 Peter 3:9).

God desires all to come into His safe, saving presence, but there is a barrier between man and God: God is holy and hates man's sin. First John 1:5 puts it this way: "God is light and in Him there is no darkness at all." As humans without Christ we are darkness and in us there is no light at all!

God is pure; apart from Christ we are not. God is incapable of sin; we are born in it. God cannot even be tempted by sin (James 1:13); we give in to temptation sometimes without batting an eyelash. God's eyes are too holy to look upon or tolerate evil (Habakkuk 1:13); we too often drool over it.

Something (or really some*one*) has to give. And I'll give you a hint: It's not God. We have to come to God on His terms, not ours.

But in another sense God is the One who gives: "For God so loved the world that He *gave* His only begotten Son, that whoever believes in Him should not perish but have eternal life" (John 3:16).

Jesus is the way. He is the highway, the high way to the Father.

Just as there was only one, precise way for the Apollo 13 spacecraft to make it through Earth's atmosphere, so there is only one way to a holy God: Jesus. He said it Himself: "I am the way and the truth and the life; no one comes to the Father but through Me" (John 14:6).

Notice that Jesus did not say he was *a way*. He said He was *the way*. Eternal life is not a cafeteria-style deal where you pick and choose the religion or religious leader that suits your taste buds that day. There is just one "meal" on the menu. You can take Him or leave Him.

Jesus said, "I am the bread of life; he who comes to Me shall not hunger, and he who believes in Me shall never thirst" (John 6:35).

Some people go through life being too busy to sit down to eat. Others take a look at the menu and walk out of the restaurant to buy some spiritual junk food elsewhere. Either way, the result is the same.

The two options for Apollo 13 if it missed the one way home were both deadly: Burn up with fire in the earth's atmosphere, or suffocate in the darkness of outer space. Either way, the result would be the same.

With a solemn warning, the Bible speaks of eternal punishment for those who reject Jesus. Hell is described both as a place of unquenchable fire and as an "outer darkness."

The Father's love is drawing you today. He longs to bring you into the safety of His arms. He wants to bring you home.

But the way home is through Jesus only. Luke recorded the apostle Peter's words which echo that theme:

> There is salvation in no one else; for there is no other name under heaven that has been given among men, by which we must be saved (Acts 4:12).

God is holy and pure and will not change. Remarkably, however, He has made a way for us to be holy and pure as well: Jesus. The Father will not budge from this one way and will not compromise for anyone. But He will forgive us of our impurity and clean out the sinful gunk from our lives so that we can come into His holy presence in prayer and enter into His holy presence for eternity in heaven.

It all happened at the cross. Jesus took the hit for us. God's holy anger that burned against sin was brutally poured out upon the body of Jesus bleeding and dying in our place.

The three men of Apollo 13 made it through Earth's atmosphere safe and sound because they were safe and sound inside the spacecraft. The spacecraft, however, didn't fare so well. Its outside was scorched, battered, and beaten up.

So was Jesus. Even though He was raised triumphantly from the dead, and given a new glorified body, He still bears the scars.

Those marks on His body will be an eternal reminder that the salvation which costs us nothing cost Jesus everything. The highway to God was not paved without pain; the highway to God was built with blood.

> A highway will be there, a roadway, and it will be called the Highway of Holiness. The unclean will not travel on it, but it will be for him who walks that way, and fools will not wander on it. No lion

will be there, nor will any vicious beast go up on it; these will not be found there. But the redeemed will walk there, and the ransomed of the LORD will return, and come with joyful shouting to Zion, with everlasting joy upon their heads. They will find gladness and joy, and sorrow and sighing will flee away (Isaiah 35:8-10).

THE LIE TO REJECT

I reject the lie that I can come to the Father on my own terms or in my own way. I refuse to believe that in my own merit I can approach God in prayer or enter eternal life.

THE TRUTH TO ACCEPT

I accept the truth that God is holy and that only through trusting in the shed blood of Jesus can I come into His holy presence. I choose to believe that Jesus' blood is sufficient to save me and make me holy and pure and able to approach God in prayer.

PRAYER FOR TODAY

Our Father, who art in heaven, hallowed and holy is Your name. I praise You for being undefiled, innocent of all evil, and so pure that You cannot even be tempted. Lord, I do believe that Jesus is the only way to You. By His death on the cross my sins are completely paid for and by His resurrection life I have eternal life. I thank You for adopting me into Your holy family and calling me Your child. You are light and there is no darkness in You at all. I choose today to walk in the light with You so that I can have sweet fellowship with You and with Your people. In Jesus' holy name I pray. Amen.

Read All About It

Isaiah 6

Going Deeper with God

Matthew 7

THE WAY UP IS DOWN

Thus says the high and exalted One who lives forever, whose name is Holy: "I dwell on a high and holy place, and also with the contrite and lowly of spirit in order to revive the spirit of the lowly and to revive the heart of the contrite" (Isaiah 57:15).

Bette Midler recorded a song a few years ago that rocketed up the charts. In it she sang these words: "God is watching us, God is watching us, God is watching us... *from a distance.*" The melody of the song was beautiful, as was the way Ms. Midler sang it. But the words were only half right.

Isaiah 57:15 tells us that God not only dwells in a high and lofty and holy place, but also with "the contrite and lowly of spirit." Unbelievable! The Most High comes to live with the most low.

Why would He do such a thing? Isn't God impressed with the great and powerful people of earth? No, as a matter of fact He's not. God will always pass by and even oppose the proud, but pour out His wonderful grace on the humble (James 4:6).

Mary, the mother of Jesus, rightly put it this way:

My soul exalts the Lord, and my spirit has rejoiced in God my Savior. For He has had regard for the humble state of His bondslave; for behold, from this time on all generations will count me blessed. For

> the Mighty One has done great things for me; and
> holy is His name. And His mercy is upon genera-
> tion after generation toward those who fear Him.
> He has done mighty deeds with His arm; He has
> scattered those who were proud in the thoughts of
> their heart. He has brought down rulers from their
> thrones, and has exalted those who were humble
> (Luke 1:46-52).

That's always the way it is with God. The first shall be last. The last shall be first. The proud shall be made low. The humble shall be exalted.

When God's people begin to admit their need for God, confess their sins to Him and to one another, and humble themselves under His mighty hand, things happen. God moves to restore, revive, refresh, and renew.

In the spring of 1995 in Christian schools, in junior and senior high youth groups, and in college campuses all over this country, God moved in a powerful way. And He did so when His people humbled themselves and prayed and began to publicly confess their sin.

The following is a testimony from the coach of a girls' basketball team, telling what God did when His people got serious about facing their sin:

> Leading a competitive women's basketball team is a chal-
> lenge on the court. But I found the off-court competition
> to be the most challenging, especially when it was between
> key players.
>
> Competition and rivalry between players for starting posi-
> tions resulted in interpersonal problems that lasted all
> through the season. One player hated being at [the school]
> and was making plans to transfer. Another was into alcohol.
> One was using drugs. Another was questioning whether

there even was a God. In spite of victories in other areas, the team was struggling internally.

Tensions continued to build throughout the year. On the second night of the campus revival meetings, three of the team members went to the microphone together [to confess their sins publicly]. Their confessions spilled out. Afterward the other team members rushed forward to pray for the three. That prayer became a turning point for our team.

That same night one key player went up to another, who she had previously seen as a threat to her position, and said, "Let's start over. I want to be friends." Later that week they were riding on a fourteen-hour road trip and having a wonderful time talking together.

A few nights later, coming to the microphone, another team member announced her new start: "I've been filled with alcohol too long, but I want to be filled with the Holy Spirit." She stuck with it. She's always been sweet, but she's a changed girl...

At the team Bible study, one renewed player read Matthew 5:8, "Blessed are the pure in heart, for they shall see God." She exclaimed, "Hello! Maybe if my heart was pure, then I could see God. We get frustrated because we say that God isn't making Himself real to us. We blame it all on God, while continuing to live a worldly life, consuming ourselves with music, movies, and all the things that are distractions during the day, instead of allowing ourselves to be consumed by the Word and by God."

That is what I think is the bottom line. You have to examine yourself, opening up to allow God to clean you out.[1]

That *is* the bottom line. Allow God to reveal the areas of impurity in your life and then allow Him to clean you out as you repent (turn away) from that sin and turn humbly back to God.

Why not take a moment right now and ask the Lord to show you if there is anything blocking your fellowship with God. Revival in your own life starts when you do the next thing God shows you to do.

THE LIE TO REJECT

I reject the lie that God is too high and mighty to ever get close to me, and that my life is too trivial to ever matter to God.

THE TRUTH TO ACCEPT

I accept the truth that the God who is holy will dwell with me as I humble myself before Him, confess my sin and pride, and admit my desperate need for Him.

PRAYER FOR TODAY

Dear heavenly Father, You have made it so clear in Your Word that You make Your home with the humble. You who are so pure that even the holy angels cover their eyes in Your presence want to live with me! As I am now in Your presence, before Your throne in prayer, would You please reveal to me anything and everything in my life that displeases You? I want to thoroughly confess it and turn away from it now. "Search me, O God, and know my heart; try me and know my anxious thoughts; and see if there be any hurtful way in me, and lead me in the everlasting way" (Psalm 139:23,24). In Jesus' name I pray. Amen.

Read All About It

Psalm 51

Going Deeper with God

Matthew 8

EAST NEVER MEETS WEST

As far as the east is from the west, so far has He removed our transgressions from us. Just as a father has compassion on his children, so the LORD has compassion on those who fear Him (Psalm 103:12,13).

My dad is not perfect. Nobody's is. He had a stressful job and was usually really tired out when he came home from work. The last thing he needed or wanted was a house full of conflict when he walked in the door each evening. Unfortunately, thanks in large part to me, that's often what he came home to find. Sometimes he blew his stack and other times he just seemed to retreat to his easy chair.

But I always knew he loved me and was committed to my well-being, come what may. I thank God for the fact that my mom and dad have stuck with their marriage for 50 years now. I felt a lot of security and safety while growing up in knowing that no matter what happened at school, they would always be at home waiting for me.

When I was a kid, one incident stands out in my mind during which my dad gave me a picture of God that I've never forgotten.

Around age ten I was really into animals. If I saw a TV show about raccoons, I'd want a raccoon for a pet. If I saw a program about foxes, I'd want one of them. I bugged my parents for everything from a skunk to a dolphin. They would just smile and wait for the next animal to come along and change my mind again.

For a long time, though, I was set on getting a horse. I had no idea how much a horse cost, but I knew it was a lot more money than I had. So I created a scheme—the "crime of the century," I thought.

One Thursday night after my dad had gotten paid at work, I carried out my plot. Mom and dad were watching TV in the living room and her purse was by the phone in the hallway, unguarded. I sneaked over and plucked a 20-dollar bill out of that purse.

On Friday after school I carried out part two of my plan. I went running down to play in the woods like I usually did. I took with me a white envelope and the 20 bucks. When I got to the woods, I put the money in the envelope and rolled it around in the dirt so it looked like it had been there awhile. A little later I came running home.

"Mom! Dad! Look what I found! I found this envelope in the woods and there was 20 dollars in it! Isn't that great?" I thought I deserved an Oscar.

"Hey, that's wonderful, dear," my mom responded. "You can use that money toward buying your horse."

Things could not have gone better. I was 20 bucks richer and my parents were none the wiser. The crime had taken place right under their noses and they suspected nothing.

The next day was Saturday and I was playing Little League baseball. My dad was sitting up on a hill watching the game. But a funny thing began to happen to me—something I hadn't planned on. Every time I looked at my dad and thought about the money I stole, I felt more and more guilty.

My conscience was ruining the whole thing!

By the time the game was over I felt terrible inside. The pressure of a guilty conscience was too much for my ten-year-old heart to bear. The closer I walked toward my dad, the more I knew I had to spill the beans.

When I reached the spot where he was sitting, I could hold it in no longer. "Dad, I didn't really find that money in the woods. I stole it out of mom's purse!" I couldn't help but cry, I felt so ashamed.

"Son, your mother and I knew that you stole that money."

I was shocked. The crime of the century had already been solved even before I confessed? Horrified, I wondered how long they had known.

"You did?" I asked in disbelief.

"Yes, son, we knew you'd stolen it, but we were just waiting for you to come and tell us."

With that, Niagara Falls erupted from my eyes. I was so sorry for what I had done and so relieved that my dad still loved me.

How did I know? He wrapped his arms around me and hugged me while I sobbed myself silly.

What a picture of our heavenly Father's forgiveness!

God knows we've sinned. There's no way to hide anything from Him. And through Christ's death on the cross He has already forgiven us for what we've done.

In His grace, the Holy Spirit works to convict us of the wrong we've done and we feel the weight of the guilt until we confess it to Him. Just like my dad, our Father is just waiting for us to come and tell him.

Then we experience His love again—a love that was always there anyway. We have that sense of His loving arms being wrapped around us, holding us and reminding us that we are and always will be His precious children.

The picture that today's Scripture gives us of the Father's forgiveness is that our sins are removed from us "as far as the east is from the west." You may have heard that phrase before, but did you ever wonder why God did not say "as far as the north is from the south"?

Well, if you travel north from where you live, eventually you will hit the North Pole and immediately start traveling south. But if you start traveling east you will continue going east until you stop.

The point is that if you went looking for your sins and journeyed east to find them, you would never get there, because west is always behind you!

In Micah 7:18,19 NIV there are more pictures of forgiveness:

> Who is a God like you, who pardons sin and forgives the transgression of the remnant of his inheritance? You do not stay angry forever but delight to show mercy. You will again have compassion on us; you will tread our sins underfoot and hurl all our iniquities into the depths of the sea.

We are pardoned, like a criminal who is set free by the judge. Our sins are trampled underfoot, crushed into the ground until we cannot see them anymore. All our evil thoughts and deeds are hurled into the deepest part of the ocean, where even Jacques Cousteau will never find them.

Are you getting the picture? God wants us to know that we are forgiven, really forgiven. Once and for all.

So the next time you're in a car headed east, take a look in the rearview mirror at the objects disappearing in the distance behind you. And remember that's how forgotten your sins are to God. For in this case, east *never* meets west.

THE LIE TO REJECT

I reject the lie that God is waiting to get back at me for my sins or that it is only a matter of time before He gets tired of my sin and gives up on me.

THE TRUTH TO ACCEPT

I accept the truth that my sins are all forgiven, once and for all. I choose to believe that my Father holds nothing against me even when my feelings tell me to feel guilt or shame. I am free!

PRAYER FOR TODAY

Dear Lord, You are so compassionate, merciful, and forgiving. When I think that You really have placed my sins as far from me as the east is from the west, it is almost too good to be true. Please help me to see that it is true, every word of it. In response to Your awesome grace, I just want to be with You and walk with You today. Enable me to show that same mercy and grace toward those who sin against me, and to hurl their sins into the deepest part of the sea of forgetfulness. In the forgiving name of Jesus, I pray. Amen.

READ ALL ABOUT IT

Psalm 103

GOING DEEPER WITH GOD

Matthew 9

JEHOVAH JIREH

*I have been young, and now I am old; Yet I have not
seen the righteous forsaken, or his descendants begging
bread* (King David in Psalm 37:25).

As I wrote the title to today's devotional, the words of
the song *Jehovah Jireh* flashed into my head. Maybe you've
sung them:

*Jehovah Jireh, my Provider, His grace is sufficient
for me.*

The melody of that song sails along joyfully and the
words are upbeat and encouraging. And rightfully so, for
the faithfulness of God is something to be glad about. What
God promises to do He always does. He always comes
through in the clutch. He has a 100 percent perfect track
record of keeping His Word.

As we see in today's Scripture verse, David had seen this
throughout his entire life, even in the toughest of times. No
doubt about it; the verdict is in: God is a Father who provides.

But do you have any idea who gave the name *Jehovah
Jireh* to God and under what circumstances? Let's turn back
to Genesis and tune in to the story:

Now it came about after these things that God
tested Abraham, and said to him, "Abraham!" And
He said, "Here I am." And He said, "Take now your

son, your only son, whom you love, Isaac, and go
to the land of Moriah; and offer him there as a burnt
offering on one of the mountains of which I will tell
you (Genesis 22:1,2).

If I had been in Abraham's sandals, I would have been
ready to write the script for the movie *The Gods Must Be
Crazy*. Poor Abraham. He had to wait 25 years for God to
fulfill His promise to give him and his wife, Sarah, a son,
and now God was telling him to kill him!

We don't know all that Abraham was feeling at this
moment, but we do know one thing: He obeyed. For three
days Abraham and his son Isaac traveled toward their
moment of truth.

Somewhere along the line Isaac sensed that something
was not quite right. He saw the fire and wood for the sacrifice, but where was the lamb?

Abraham assured his son that God Himself would provide the lamb. And as far as Abraham knew at that point,
that lamb was walking next to him carrying the wood.

So the two walked on together. Isaac no doubt was filled
with a sense of adventure and joy just being with his dad.
He was curious about what they would use for a sacrifice,
but his dad's answer had satisfied him for the moment.
Abraham, however, was likely deep in thought, battling his
own sense of grief and loss with each step closer to the mountain.

What kept Abraham from going crazy? Why didn't he
just shake his fist at God, throw down the knife, wood, and
fire, grab his son's hand, and run? Hang on, the answer's
coming!

When the two finally arrived at the place God had told
them, Abraham built an altar, arranged the wood on it, tied
up Isaac, and placed him on top of the wood (Genesis 22:9).

By this time Isaac must have thought both God and his dad had gone completely off the deep end. As Abraham raised the knife to plunge it into Isaac's chest, that young man no doubt squinted his eyes tightly closed, trying to shut out the unbelievable horror that was happening to him.

And then the voice came from heaven, like the governor's phone call with a last-minute reprieve of a criminal on death row. "Abraham, Abraham!" the angel of the LORD called, and stopped him from sacrificing his son.

And suddenly it was all over. The test was finished. Abraham (and Isaac!) had passed with flying colors. God had not gone crazy. Abraham's precious boy was still alive.

Abraham looked up and there was the sacrifice, a ram with its horns caught in a thicket. He offered that animal as a burnt offering to the Lord in place of Isaac. And then Abraham gave that place a name: *Jehovah Jireh*, which means "The LORD will provide."

How was Abraham able to pass such a severe test? Hebrews 11:17,19 gives the faith-filled answer:

> By faith Abraham, when he was tested, offered up Isaac; and he who had received the promises was offering up his only begotten son.... He considered that God is able to raise men even from the dead..."

That's bottom-line faith.

One thing I have learned in 24 years of walking with God is this: *God is never late, but He's rarely early!* The Lord is faithful. He always provides what we need when we *need* it. But He doesn't often provide it when we *want* it—which is usually five minutes ago!

We get into trouble and suffer anger, anxiety, frustration, and even depression when we fall into this trap:

Trying to figure out how God should meet our need
and when He ought to do it.

One of the hardest lessons you'll ever learn is that *He is
God and you are not!* When we stop trying to play God by
trying to figure out how everything will work out, we experience peace. But when we try to dictate to God what He
should do or try to manipulate Him by our prayers, we hit
a brick wall.

God simply cannot and will not give in to our demands.
He cannot be bargained with, bribed, bullied, threatened,
tricked, or convinced against His will.

Every scheme and strategy that may work great with
your parents will fall flat on its face before God. Frustrating
as it may seem, God is the one Person in the entire universe
over whom you have absolutely no control.

God alone does what He wants when He wants with
whom He wants. That's one of the things that makes Him
God.

So stop fighting and start "faithing." Recognize today
that God is indeed *Jehovah Jireh,* your provider. His grace is
sufficient for you. In the end you'll look back on how He
met your needs and you'll shake your head in amazement.
It will be far better than you could ever have concocted yourself.

Just ask Abraham and Isaac.

THE LIE TO REJECT

*I reject the devil's lie that God doesn't love me and can't
be trusted. I refuse to set up my own test of God's love
and then get angry with Him when He doesn't give me
my way.*

The Truth to Accept

I accept the truth that God is indeed Jehovah Jireh, my provider. I choose to believe that truth even when He doesn't do things the way I think He should. He is God and I am not.

Prayer for Today

Dear Lord, I know I have many times tied myself up in emotional knots because I thought I had You all figured out, and then You changed my rules. I became frustrated and angry . Forgive me for the times I have used everything in my bag of tricks to try to get You to do my will. Right now I say to You, Lord, "Not my will, but Thine be done." I thank You that You are faithful and that You have never been unfaithful, even for one instant. I choose to trust You today with (name the things that are on your heart), *leaving the solution in Your hands. I'm grateful that You cannot be manipulated, because then You would not be God and I would really be on my own. I pray all these things with gratitude and faith in Jesus' name. Amen.*

Read All About It

Genesis 22

Going Deeper with God

Matthew 10

WHEN GOD PLAYS HARDBALL

Naked I came from my mother's womb, and naked I shall return there. The LORD gave and the LORD has taken away. Blessed be the name of the LORD (Job 1:21).

God doesn't play by our rules. Our rules basically come down to this one rule: *I deserve to be happy.* God's rules basically come down to this one rule: *I will make you like my Son, Jesus. In the end, that will bring the greatest happiness, but for now it may not be easy.*

A couple on our staff, Brian and Anne, could write a book on that subject. Maybe someday they will. For now, here are some excerpts from Anne's journal:

> On Monday (today is Saturday) we owe three house payments or they are probably going to start proceedings to take the house. The credit union is turning us over to their attorney on Monday unless they get over $800 to catch us up on the car payments. Our other car broke down and that car is still sitting at the gas station because we can't deal with trying to fix it or tow it yet.
>
> I now don't have a stove to cook with. Our money is gone and we don't have food for the next two weeks except what is left in the refrigerator and cupboard. I have a ham the church donated to us, but can't cook it because of the stove. It is our only real meat for next week, so we are going to try and cut it in half and cook it in our Crock-Pot. I'm

making up a Crock-Pot full of meat and beans today, which hopefully will last us a couple of days.

Besides our house and car being in danger, we will have our heat and other utilities cut off if we can't bring our bills up to date.

Our son hasn't had a doctor visit for 11 months. He is getting behind on shots. Brian needs his shoulder operated on, and three teeth crowned, and now his heel is bothering him as well.[1]

There's more going on, but time and space don't allow us to include it all. How are they managing through it all? Anne's frank diary continues:

Lord Jesus, please help us. I don't know why He is allowing this to happen. We KNOW we are called to this ministry and will continue in it no matter what.

The truth is life-giving and we know we are called to share this message. God's truth and freedom override the physical needs of this old world. We will go on, we will persevere. We will have faith.

Brian and I have become the servants of Jesus Christ in a deeper way than ever before. As we die to ourselves and the materialism and "seen" things of this world, it hurts, but our prayer is that Jesus Christ may be glorified.[2]

You will be encouraged to know that through generous gifts and a ministry location change (resulting in much lower living expenses), things are looking up for Brian and Anne. I guess we could say that "things are looking up for them because they never *stopped* looking up!"

Today's Scripture was spoken by Job, a godly man who suffered the loss of his children, his possessions, and his health. And although he went through a painful time of questioning God, and had to be humbled, Job never denied his faith. The apostle James commends him by writing:

> Behold, we count those blessed who endured. You have heard of the endurance of Job and have seen the outcome of the Lord's dealings, that the Lord is full of compassion and is merciful (James 5:11).

Indeed, God was merciful to Job. He eventually restored his health and wealth and blessed him with even more children than had before.

What was Job's secret? He knew that everything he had belonged to God. Notice his words:

> Naked I came from my mother's womb, and naked I shall return there.

Job knew that he had entered this world with nothing and he would exit it the same way.

> The LORD gave and the LORD has taken away.

Job's natural (and correct) conclusion was that everything he had was given to him by God and therefore God had every right to take it back whenever He saw fit.

That flies right in the face of our American way of life. We are a nation built on the "Bill of Rights." We declare that everyone in this country is "endowed" with certain "inalienable rights," including the right to life, liberty, and the pursuit of happiness.

Everywhere you turn you hear about the right to live, the right to die, the right to choose, the right to privacy, civil rights, gay rights, animal rights, and so on.

But is all our focus on "rights" right?

When it comes to our relationship with God, we are in no position to *demand* anything. We cannot tell God what He can and cannot do.

We are God's *children*, dependent upon the goodness and grace of our heavenly Father. We are God's *servants*, called to follow Him and do what He asks of us. We are God's *sheep*, in need of being led by the Shepherd to feed and rest our bodies and souls.

It may not be today or this week or even this year, but you can guarantee that sometime and probably many times in your life, God will throw you a curve. He won't do it to be mean, but to be merciful.

Merciful? How can tough times be a sign of God's mercy? Because during the times our faith is tested the gunk in our lives floats to the surface and is skimmed away by God. Then we shine even brighter, with a faith more precious than gold (see 1 Peter 1).

So what do you do when God plays hardball?

In the midst of the pain and suffering, remember that God will always be merciful, even when He's tough. What was Job's reaction? He cried out through his tears:

> "Blessed be the name of the LORD." Through all this Job did not sin nor did he blame God.

Job passed the test. So did Brian and Anne. May we pass the test as well.

The Lie to Reject

I reject the lie that the Christian life is always a happy, carefree life. I refuse to demand my right to be happy and have things go my way.

THE TRUTH TO ACCEPT

I accept the truth that God's primary desire for me is to become like Jesus. And since He learned obedience through what He suffered, so will I. I accept hardship and suffering as a part of God's perfect plan for my life.

PRAYER FOR TODAY

Dear Father, I have to admit that, like most Americans, I'm pretty spoiled. I expect to be able to take a pill and have all my pain go away. But life isn't like that, and I don't want to make demands of You for an easy, happy life. Lord, all Your choice servants, including Job, went through tough times. Jesus went through the toughest of all. Help me to trust in You and rest in You when the going gets rough. I thank You that You will not allow more in my life than I can handle (1 Corinthians 10:13). May I come through the trials in my life as purified gold. In Jesus' strong name and for His glory I pray. Amen.

READ ALL ABOUT IT

Job 1,2

GOING DEEPER WITH GOD

Matthew 11

DAY TWELVE

TORNADO!

The LORD is slow to anger and great in power; the LORD will not leave the guilty unpunished. His way is in the whirlwind and the storm, and clouds are the dust of his feet (Nahum 1:3 NIV).

Tornado warning! The words send chills up and down the spines of normally brave people. On the average, around 100,000 thunderstorms hit the U.S. each year, 10,000 of them being severe, and nearly 1000 of them producing tornadoes.

The greatest risk is during the period of April to July in what is known as Tornado Alley—from north-central Texas through the central parts of Oklahoma, Kansas, Nebraska, and the Dakotas. But tornadoes can show up in any month of the year,[1] in almost any location.

In Georgia, the peak season for tornadoes is early spring, when cold, dry air from the Northwest clashes with warm, humid air from the Gulf of Mexico. A strong subtropical jet stream adds the upper-air energy to fuel the twisters.

In the spring of 1993 my pregnant wife, my daughter and I were staying at my in-laws' house in Lawrenceville, Georgia. A tornado watch had been issued and I watched the supercell thunderstorm approach the area. It was nearly midnight as the storm marched closer and closer, the frequent lightning flashes more awesome than any fireworks.

My family thought I was a little extreme as I herded them into the downstairs hallway, huddled against an interior wall away from the windows.

Knowing the destructive damage of tornadic winds, at times well over 200 miles per hour, I prayed. The others were downstairs giggling and enjoying the moment. I was very concerned.

To my relief, the thunderstorm veered away, giving Lawrenceville a mere glancing blow. I watched and listened as it boomed its way off into the distance, like an angry giant stomping through the night.

The small town of Grayson, Georgia (just a few miles away), was not so lucky. A tornado spawned by that thunderstorm struck a house, killing a little girl who had been visiting from Missouri.

The power of tornadoes is almost beyond belief. Some have been a mile across and have traveled for hundreds of miles before snaking back up into the cloud from which they came. Those are unusual, however, with the average life span of a twister being only ten minutes or so.

On April 3-4, 1974, our nation's midsection experienced the largest, most damaging outbreak of tornadoes in recorded history. Half the town of Xenia, Ohio, just east of Dayton, was wiped off the map.

During those two days a plague of 127 tornadoes broke out in 11 states. When it was over, 315 people had died, 6142 were injured, and property damage reached 600 million dollars. At least six of the twisters had winds of over 261 miles per hour, the strongest category of tornadoes.

At one school in Xenia, a teacher and students were on stage in the auditorium practicing for a play. When the tornado warning was issued, they fled from the building just seconds before the twister tossed two school buses through the wall of the auditorium and onto the stage.[2]

Why does God allow such devastating storms?

Nahum 1:3 first gives us comfort by saying, "The LORD is slow to anger." It is clear that God is not hot-tempered, flying into a rage at the slightest provocation. He is slow to get angry.

But He is also "great in power" and "will not leave the guilty unpunished." Sometimes God uses the forces of nature to teach the human race a lesson. We all need a reminder once in a while that God is *all-powerful*. At times like that "His way is in the whirlwind and the storm, and clouds are the dust of his feet."

Does this mean that those who die in storms are bad people and those who are spared are good? We all wish it were that easy, but it's not. God's ways are much more mysterious than that. We want simplistic answers to questions like this, but they simply do not exist.

Jesus dealt with this issue in Luke 13 when He gave His color commentary on the top news stories of that day:

> Now on the same occasion there were some present who reported to Him about the Galileans, whose blood Pilate had mingled with their sacrifices. And He answered and said to them, "Do you suppose that these Galileans were greater sinners than all other Galileans, because they suffered this fate? I tell you, no, but unless you repent you will all likewise perish. Or do you suppose that those eighteen on whom the tower of Siloam fell and killed them were worse culprits than all the men who live in Jerusalem? I tell you, no, but unless you repent you will all likewise perish" (Luke 13:1-5).

So what lesson does God want to teach us through the storms, whirlwinds, and tornadoes? "The LORD is slow to anger and great in power; the LORD will not leave the guilty unpunished. His way is in the whirlwind and the storm" (Nahum 1:3 NIV).

What we ought to do is tremble before the power of Almighty God and give thanks for His mercy. Know that the tornado, in all its power and fury, represents but a whisper of God's great strength.

We should also bow before His majesty and mystery, realizing there are some things beyond our ability to understand. We dare not judge those who are victims. If there is any judging to be done, that is God's business, not ours.

He will handle all of that in His time and will make everything right at the time of judgment. Until then, the reality is that bad things happen to good people, and good things happen to bad people.

We should ask the Lord to examine our own hearts, and if necessary, we should repent.

The Lie to Reject

I reject the lie that God is fully predictable and that we as humans can figure out and understand all His ways. I refuse to listen to the pride that would cause me to judge others.

The Truth to Accept

I accept the truth that God is great in power and that His power is awesome and mysterious, beyond my ability to fully grasp. I choose to believe that, though not all things make sense to me on earth, God is good and just and will one day make everything right.

Prayer for Today

Dear heavenly Father, I thank You that You are slow to anger. Many times I have done things that greatly displeased You, and yet by Your grace I still live and You still love me. I am so grateful for Your mercy. As I look at the power of nature, and realize that it is just a tiny fraction of Your mighty strength, I tremble before You. Forgive me for the times I have seen You as weak or powerless. You are the Almighty God and I humble myself before You and bow in Your awesome presence. In Jesus' name. Amen.

Read All About It

Nahum 1

Going Deeper with God

Matthew 12

I COULDN'T GET OUT OF MY SEAT!

The Spirit of the Lord is upon Me, because He anointed Me to preach the gospel to the poor. He has sent Me to proclaim release to the captives, and recovery of sight to the blind, to set free those who are downtrodden, to proclaim the favorable year of the Lord" (Luke 4:18,19).

I'm convinced that we are largely unaware of what God is doing around us in people's lives. We often cannot see His power at work because it is operating quietly, deep inside the heart. Sometimes that discourages us from speaking up about our faith, because nothing seems to happen when we do. But once in a while the Lord yanks back the curtains and gives us a bright picture of what He's up to. One of those times came at a conference for college students at which I was one of the speakers.

After my message on forgiving others from the heart, a young man, Phil, came up to me and asked if I could talk with his friend Jonathan.

When I walked over to where Jonathan was seated, he was sobbing so hard that we couldn't understand a word he was trying to say. We just had to sit back and wait for him to calm down. Eventually we figured out that he had been deeply hurt by his dad cutting him down. He was also very upset that his dad had committed adultery.

After a bit of encouragement, Jonathan was able to let go of the anger and hatred he felt and sincerely forgave his dad for those things.

In Luke 4:18,19 (the Scripture at the beginning of the chapter), Jesus promised that He had come to "set free those who are downtrodden." He was doing that before our very eyes. Jonathan had been beaten down emotionally because of the abuse and pain caused by his father, but Jesus set him free that day.

That was remarkable enough, but God had done something supernatural to bring him to the point of forgiveness.

Three days later I found out what had happened. After concluding a seminar for guys on "God's View of Sexuality," Jonathan came up and told me.

In my earlier message on forgiveness, I had used the parable of the Prodigal Son as a basis for an invitation for the students to come back to God. That didn't sit well with Jonathan.

"I have hated that parable," he confessed, "because everybody uses it and I've heard it so much!" From the tone of his voice, I had no doubt that Jonathan meant what he was saying.

Wanting to get out of the meeting as fast as possible, so he wouldn't have to listen to that hated parable, Jonathan encountered a problem he hadn't expected.

"I couldn't get out of my seat!" he shouted, eyes bulging.

I just smiled. Later on I imagined this angel casually floating in the air above Jonathan with one finger pressing down on the top of his head.

But that wasn't all God did during that conference to "proclaim release to the captives, and recovery of sight to the blind."

In Jonathan's case, He had moved with His powerful healing hand upon an individual. On the afternoon of New Year's Eve, He swept over a group.

It happened at the end of that guys' sexuality seminar I mentioned earlier. I had felt an unusual stirring in my spirit the day before, prompting me to ask God if He had anything special in mind. An idea began to take shape in my head.

I felt that the Lord would have me give an invitation to the 220 or so college guys to come forward to deal with the sexual sin in their lives. A twinge of fear hit me: *Is this from God or just me? Will anyone come forward?*

I decided to take the risk.

So many young people are trapped in sexual sin, and through 900 numbers and the Internet, pornography is easy to find. Knowing those things, I felt I needed to provide some help and hope to those guys.

As I concluded my message I said, "Many of you have committed secret sin, have felt secret shame and guilt, and are now struggling with secret defeat in your Christian lives. Private confession hasn't worked. James 5:16 says to 'confess your sins to one another, and pray for one another, so that you may be healed. The effective prayer of a righteous man can accomplish much.'

"Isn't it time for you to find the freedom that Christ came to give? In a moment I'm going to invite you to come forward to confess your sin publicly. Look around the room, find a trusted friend, and bring him with you. He will pray for you as you confess your sin."

After a brief prayer, I made the invitation and sat down. Then the floodgates opened. For 20 minutes or so the front of the room was filled with around 175 young men confessing sexual sin and praying for each other. It was beautiful. It was God at work.

After everyone had finished and returned to their seats, we all prayed out loud together, thanking God for His powerful forgiveness and cleansing in our lives. I shared with them the story of the woman caught in adultery in John 8 and reminded them of Jesus' words to her:

> Neither do I condemn you. . . . From now on sin no more.

Then I sat down, drained but exhilarated.

What happened next blew me away. Spontaneously, the whole crowd rose to their feet, applauding, whooping, and cheering (as only college guys can do!). What a moment of victory and freedom and joy! My heart nearly burst with gratitude for what God had done in the lives of His children.

Have you been caught in some sin, maybe even a sexual one? Have you silently confessed that sin over and over again but seem to have no power to overcome its hold on your life?

For some sins, it's enough to confess it privately to God. First John 1:9 says, "If we confess our sins, He is faithful and righteous to forgive us our sins and to cleanse us from all unrighteousness." Once we do that, we can get up and move on with our lives, clean and free.

But for sin that has become a habit, often we need help from a brother or sister in Christ (preferably of our own gender).

Is that how you are struggling today? You probably won't see the power of God unleashed in setting you free until you humble yourself and get help from someone. Confess your sin to that person and ask him to pray for you.

Like Jonathan or that group of guys, you will find that "the effective prayer of a righteous man can accomplish much" (James 5:16).

For help in overcoming sexual sin, work through the following exercise in the presence of a trusted Christian friend. Start out by praying out loud:

> *Lord, I ask You to reveal to my mind every sexual use of my body as an instrument of unrighteousness. In Jesus' precious name I pray. Amen.*

As the Lord brings to your mind every wrong sexual use of your body, whether it was done to you (i.e. rape, incest, sexual abuse, or molestation) or willingly by you (i.e. habitual masturbation, homosexual sin, pornography, sexual foreplay or intercourse outside of marriage), *renounce every occasion* out loud:

> *Lord, I renounce (name the specific use of your body) with (name any other person involved) and I ask You to break that sinful bond with (name).*

After you have completed this exercise, commit your body to the Lord by praying out loud from your heart:

Lord, I renounce all these uses of my body as an instrument of unrighteousness, and I admit to my willful participation. Lord, I choose to present my eyes, my mouth, my hands, my feet, my sexual organs, and my entire body to You as instruments of righteousness. I now present my body to You as a living sacrifice, holy and acceptable unto You, and I choose to reserve the sexual use of my body for marriage only (Hebrews 13:4).

I reject the lie of Satan that my body is not clean or that it is dirty or in any way unacceptable to You as a result of my past sexual experiences. Lord, I thank You that You have totally cleansed and forgiven me, and that You love me just as I am. Therefore I can accept myself and my body as cleansed in Your eyes. In Jesus' name. Amen.[1]

Read All About It

Romans 6

Going Deeper with God

Matthew 13

What's in a Name?

The name of the LORD is a strong tower; the righteous runs into it and is safe (Proverbs 18:10).

Things happen when you start talking about Jesus. You can talk about "God" or even "the Lord" and not rock the boat. You could even drop the names of other religious leaders in a conversation, like Buddha, Muhammad, Confucius, etc., and not get a reaction.

But mention the name of Jesus (in a positive, not cursing way!) and look out!

When I was in youth ministry in Southern California, I took a high school student with me one evening on a "cross-cultural" missions trip. I decided to take Daniel to a Chinese restaurant.

We had a good meal and were getting ready to leave when I suggested to him, "Hey, let's try to talk to the owner about Jesus." He agreed, so we walked up together to pay him for the dinner.

"Sir, this has been a wonderful meal and we're grateful to you. In return we would like to do something for you." I was pleasantly smiling at the man, watching the curiosity grow and show on his face. I continued, "We would like to tell you about *Jesus*."

Immediately the man's face changed. He frowned and began to wave his arms in the air. "Ah, no!" he shouted.

"No! No! NO!" And with that he handed us our change and rushed back into the kitchen.

Daniel and I just stood there for a moment looking at each other. Then we shrugged our shoulders and left.

You just never know what will happen when you use that name. We were about to find that out in a way we would never have expected.

By the time we left the Chinese restaurant it was after nine o'clock at night. For some goofy reason I had decided we should walk the mile or so from Daniel's house to the restaurant, so we began our walk back. The road we were walking down was a main road but poorly lit and lightly traveled at that time of evening.

After a couple of minutes we heard a voice shouting from down a side street.

"Hey, you white dudes!"

I kept on chatting with Daniel, hoping the guy was yelling at someone else. Inside, though, a chill of fear began to freeze my gut. My gut-level instincts proved right.

"HEY, YOU WHITE DUDES! STOP!" The voice was louder and more insistent this time.

I told Daniel, "I guess we'd better stop because we're the only white dudes around here." I'm sure Daniel must have been vowing never to go anywhere with me again!

Once we stopped, we were immediately surrounded by a group of five Hispanic young men with knives menacingly pointed toward us.

I could see the headlines already in tomorrow morning's paper: "TWO WHITE DUDES BECOME HUMAN SPRINKLER SYSTEMS." I braced myself and prayed.

The same guy, who must've been their leader, started explaining their actions. "Some white dudes have been messing with my sister."

"We don't know your sister," I replied, calmly looking the leader in the eye.

"Well," he stammered a little bit, "some white dudes have been messing with my sister." He was obviously not prepared for my brilliant response.

"Listen, we don't know your sister, and even if we did we wouldn't mess with her. You see, we're Christians, followers of Jesus, and we wouldn't do that.

"My name is Rich and this is Daniel. Do you know what the name 'Daniel' means?" I paused, waiting for the response I knew would come. The five guys shook their heads. "Daniel means 'God is judge,' and if you lay a hand on us, God will judge *you!*"

I couldn't believe those words had come out of my mouth. I concluded I was either insane or inspired. Their reaction still amazes me to this day.

It was like some weird spell that had hung over the five guys was broken. They immediately put away their knives and started introducing themselves!

"Rich, I'm pleased to meet you. My name is José. I live in Casablanca."

"Glad to meet you, José. I've been to Casablanca, talking to your neighbors about Jesus."

"Oh really? That's great."

And on and on. In quick succession all the five guys shook our hands and told us their names. In the end we had a very nice visit with those young men.

Then as quickly as they had come, they were gone. Off to look for some other "white dudes," I suppose.

Daniel and I walked the rest of the way home—at a fast pace! — rejoicing at God's saving hand and at the power of the name of Jesus.

Now obviously, God had led us into those incidents to teach us some lessons, one of which was not to walk on dark streets at night! But beyond that, He wanted us to see that spiritual battles rage and are won through the name of Jesus.

I'm not saying that the name of Jesus is a magic wand that will keep you from all harm. We dare not put the Lord to the test by placing ourselves in dangerous situations on purpose, trying to force God to save us. That would be a terrible sin.

But when God allows *us* to be tested and we find ourselves in need of help, call out for Jesus, and do it out loud. Why? *The name of the Lord is a strong tower; the righteous runs into it and is safe.*

Here are 30 titles among the many that the Bible uses to describe Jesus. In what way do you need to trust in the strong name of Jesus Christ? Chances are you'll find the strength you need in one of His names. Read the list of names out loud and look up the Scriptures next to your favorite ones.

Deliverer *(Romans 11:26)*

Good Shepherd *(John 10:11)*

Guardian of Souls *(1 Peter 2:25)*

High Priest *(Hebrews 4:14)*

Chief Shepherd *(1 Peter 5:4)*

Resurrection and Life *(John 11:25)*

Lamb of God *(John 1:29)*

Light of the World *(John 8:12)*

King of kings *(Revelation 17:14)*

Son of God *(Romans 1:4)*

Lord Jesus Christ *(1 Peter 1:3)*

Lord of lords *(Revelation 17:14)*

Prince of Peace *(Isaiah 9:6)*

Ruler *(Matthew 2:6)*

Beloved *(Ephesians 1:6)*

Bread of Life *(John 6:35)*

Holy One *(1 John 2:20)*

Counselor *(Isaiah 9:6)*

Mighty God *(Isaiah 9:6)*

Rock *(1 Corinthians 10:4)*

Truth *(John 14:6)*

Savior *(Luke 2:11)*

Son of Man *(Matthew 24:30)*

Teacher *(John 13:13)*

Way *(John 14:6)*

Life *(John 14:6)*

Word of God *(Revelation 19:13)*   Redeemer *(Isaiah 59:20)*
Faithful and True *(Revelation 19:11)*   Author and Perfecter of
Faith *(Hebrews 12:2)*

PRAYER FOR TODAY

Dear Lord, how awesome is Your name! I praise Your holy name and choose to run into that strong tower today so I can be safe from my enemies. Help me to remember Your name, Jesus, and all the titles that describe who You are. When I encounter difficult problems and confusing circumstances, I want to rest in Your strong name. I thank You that "God highly exalted Him, and bestowed on Him the name which is above every name, that at the name of Jesus every knee should bow ... and that every tongue should confess that Jesus Christ is Lord, to the glory of God the Father." And it is all in that name, Jesus, I pray. Amen.

READ ALL ABOUT IT

Philippians 2

GOING DEEPER WITH GOD

Matthew 14

PATIENCE CARRIES A LOT OF WAIT

The LORD longs to be gracious to you, and therefore He waits on high to have compassion on you. For the LORD is a God of justice; How blessed are all those who long for Him (Isaiah 30:18).

Today's title was inspired by a sign I saw on a church message board: "Patience is a virtue that carries a lot of wait"

The Bible teaches that "love is patient" (1 Corinthians 13:4). In fact, in that famous "love chapter" is a whole list of things that love is and is not, does and does not. And guess which one is first? "Love is patient."

Do you want a good test of how much you love people? Check to see how patient you are with them. Are you always nagging and pushing them to change, finding yourself more and more irritated with their slowness?

Why not pause for a moment and ask the Lord to take you through the "love is patient" test. How are you doing in the area of patience with your parents? Teachers? Brothers and sisters? Friends? Boyfriend or girlfriend? Yourself?

If you're like me, you'll have to honestly admit that you're the least patient with the people you're closest to.

I'm so glad that God is not that way with us. How do I know that? Because "God is love" (1 John 4:8) and "love is patient" (1 Corinthians 13:4).

What is patience? Patience is the desire and ability to wait for people to change, while loving them enough to accept them even when they don't!

That kind of patience only comes from God, because God is gracious and compassionate. No matter how many times we fall and fail, God does not give up on us. He continues to pour out His patient love toward us long after the most noble human friend would have thrown up his hands in frustration.

Does that mean God is soft on sin? I hope you don't think so, especially after our devotionals on His holiness. No, God hates sin. He hates yours and He hates mine.

But He also patiently bears with our weakness, drawing (not driving!) us back to Himself and nudging (not nagging!) us to allow Him to change us.

That's a love I can live with.

When I think of how God dealt patiently with His people in the Bible, certain names pop right into mind—Peter, Mark, Aaron, David, Job, and others.

Today, however, I want to introduce you to another guy. His name is Jerubbaal. Ever heard of him? Probably not by that name. You might know him better as Gideon.

When the angel of the LORD first came to Gideon, he was hiding out in the wine press, trying to thresh some wheat. He was afraid the Midianites would come and steal it, something they had done all over the country. The Israelites had been oppressed by Midian for seven years.

"The LORD is with you, O valiant warrior," the angel said to the young man.

Gideon then took the opportunity to complain to the angel about how God was not with them at all, but had abandoned them to the Midianites.

Gideon should have known he was being set up.

The angel basically replied, "Well, then, go do something about it! I will send you to deliver Israel."

That was not the answer Gideon had expected. He protested, "O Lord, how shall I deliver Israel? Behold, my family is the least in Manasseh, and I am the youngest in my father's house."

Translation? "God, with all due respect, You've got the wrong man. After all, I come from the wrong side of the tracks. We don't have much money, and besides, look at me! I'm just a teenager!"

But God had already made up His mind. In essence God said, "Nope, Gideon, you're the man. I'll be with you and you'll defeat the enemy."

As you can see, God had already shown some patience with Gideon. After all, how many people have the spunk to argue with an angel in the first place? But God was just getting warmed up in the patience department, because Gideon had a tough time really believing God was going to use him.

It should have been enough that the angel of the LORD told Gideon that God would deliver Israel through Gideon— especially when the angel touched the food Gideon gave him with his staff and caused fire to leap from a rock to consume the meal! I mean, what greater proof do you need?

But then Gideon decided he wanted to conduct a scientific experiment to prove God was with him. On two nights in a row he put a fleece of wool out on the ground, and asked God to do him a favor. During the first night he wanted God to put dew on the fleece but not on the ground.

And that's what God did. But was that good enough for Gideon? Nooooo!

The next night he wanted God to do the opposite—dry fleece, wet ground. And God did that for him, too.

What patience! By that time I would have had it with the boy and told him to forget it. But not God.

Later on, Gideon got a little nervous again about whether they were really going to win this battle. And I can understand his feelings: He had 300 men with torches, clay pots, and trumpets while the enemy troops "were lying in the valley as numerous as locusts; and their camels were without number, as numerous as the sand on the seashore" (Judges 7:12).

So God patiently cut Gideon some slack again. He told him to go down to the enemy camp and listen. When he did he overheard one guy telling his buddy about a dream he had. His friend interpreted the dream by saying:

> This is nothing less than the sword of Gideon, the son of Joash, a man of Israel; God has given Midian and all the camp into his hand (Judges 7:14).

Finally Gideon was convinced, and God used him to rout the enemy. But God had to tell Gideon at least six times that He would use Him to deliver Israel before the young man cried out to the Israelite soldiers:

> Arise, for the LORD has given the camp of Midian into your hands (Judges 7:15).

Do you ever feel like God is sick and tired of trying to teach you the same lesson over and over again? Do you ever wonder if God is about give up on you and find someone else who learns faster? Do you ever get the picture in your mind that God is looking at you and just shaking His head muttering to Himself, "When is this kid ever going to get it?"

If you have, welcome to the human race. Somewhere along the line each one of us feels that way, especially when we've done something really dumb.

Well, the next time you feel like God is about to throw in the towel and trade you in for another model, remember Gideon.

Better yet, remember God. He is patient, longing to be gracious to you and waiting on high to have compassion on you. In other words, God loves *you*. And love is patient.

THE LIE TO REJECT

I reject the lie that God has given up on me or is about to. I refuse to believe the enemy's accusations that I am worthless, inadequate, or useless to God.

THE TRUTH TO ACCEPT

I accept the truth that God is patient with me, compassionate and gracious. I choose to believe the truth that God loves me enough to wait for me to change and accepts me even when I don't.

PRAYER FOR TODAY

Dear heavenly Father, I know there are so many times when I doubt or disbelieve Your Word. There are areas in my life that I struggle with so much day after day. It's easy to imagine that You are really fed up with me. But thank You for showing me that You are patient, compas-

sionate, and gracious. You love me just the way I am. And even though You are totally committed to my becoming like Jesus, You don't nag or push. You gently draw me to Yourself so You can change me. And even when I'm afraid of letting You work in me, You patiently love me. I want to give You my full permission now to do in me and through me all that You desire. In Jesus' name. Amen.

Read All About It

Judges 6,7

Going Deeper with God

Matthew 15

Day Sixteen

Unclean! Unclean!

*Moved with compassion, He stretched out His hand
and touched him, and said to him, I am willing; be
cleansed* (Mark 1:41).

I hope I can meet Mother Teresa someday—someday
when I'm really feeling down, when I'm feeling like all the
ugliness and pain and suffering of the world have decided
to hold their annual convention in the pit of my stomach.

A number of years ago on Christmas Eve she was on
CNN. This tiny woman with a big heart had her arms
wrapped around two skeletal-looking AIDS patients. They
had been released that day from a state penitentiary in New
York to come live in a home started by Mother Teresa's order.

During the CNN interview a reporter harshly asked,
"Why should we care about criminals with AIDS?"

Mother Teresa calmly replied that young men like the
two she was hugging had been created in the image of God
and deserved to know His love. [1]

Charles Colson happened to catch that broadcast. He
wrote in his powerful book *The Body*: "I went to sleep that
night thinking about Mother Teresa, and at the same time
thanking God that I didn't have to deal with AIDS patients." [2]

The next day Mr. Colson was preaching in a women's
prison when the warden asked if he would like to visit Bessie
Shipp. Bessie had AIDS. After fumbling through a few

excuses, he finally agreed to see her. Somehow the words of Mother Teresa would not let him out of their grasp.

He described his meeting with her:

> A chill came over me as we swung open the gate to the isolation cell, where a petite young woman sat bundled up in a bathrobe, reading a Bible. She looked up, and her eyes brightened as the chaplain said, "I promised I'd bring you a Christmas present, Bessie."
>
> We chatted for a few moments, and since there wasn't much time for either of us, I decided I had better get to the point.
>
> "Bessie, do you know Jesus?" I asked.
>
> "No," she said. "I try to. I read this book. I want to know Him, but I haven't been able to find Him."
>
> "We can settle it right now," I said, taking her hand. The chaplain took her other hand, and together we led Bessie in prayer. When we finished, she looked at us with tears flowing down her cheeks. It was a life-changing moment for Bessie—and for me. [3]

A pastor friend of mind told me of a conversation he had with the mother of a young man who had recently died of AIDS. Unfortunately, he found out about the man's death two weeks too late.

Here is the short conversation she had with her dying son:

> "Mom, do you think I'll go to hell for what I've done?"
>
> "I don't know, dear, but I bet a minister would know. Do you want me to call a minister for you to talk to?"

"No," he said sadly, shaking his head, "I don't think a minister would want to talk to someone like me."

Jesus was traveling throughout the region of Galilee, preaching and casting out demons from people. Mark 1:40-42 tells us what happened next:

> And a leper came to Him, beseeching Him and falling on his knees before Him, and saying to Him, "If You are willing, You can make me clean." And moved with compassion, He stretched out His hand and touched him, and said to him, "I am willing; be cleansed." And immediately the leprosy left him and he was cleansed.

The leper's behavior was highly unusual, for leprosy was so contagious that strict rules were instituted to keep the disease isolated. For example, look at what Leviticus 13:45,46 NIV commands:

> The person with such an infectious disease must wear torn clothes, let his hair be unkempt, cover the lower part of his face and cry out, "Unclean! Unclean!" As long as he has the infection he remains unclean. He must live alone; he must live outside the camp.

Unclean. Isolated. Alone. Feared. Unwanted. The poor leper who came to Jesus must have been absolutely desperate.

Why do you imagine that Mark 1 talks about the leper coming just to Jesus? Where do you think the disciples were? We can't say for sure, but I can easily picture them all running to save their skins as soon as they saw that renegade leper approach.

But Jesus didn't run.

The disciples must have gasped in horror when Jesus reached out and touched the man. You can almost read their thoughts:

Oh no! He's gone too far this time! He's touching him! He's going to get leprosy Himself! Then what will happen to us? He's ruining everything!

But Jesus had to touch him, because He was "moved with compassion." Literally this meant that Jesus' heart was so touched by the man's condition that his insides were torn up with pity. He had to do something, and so He cleansed the man of his leprosy.

What else would you expect of Jesus? He was a man of compassion. He cared *about* people so He cared *for* people.

You and I may not have the opportunity to hug a leprosy or an AIDS patient, but then again, with the way things are going, maybe we will.

What about the lonely, isolated outcasts around us? The kids in school who don't fit in? The ones who dress funny or act "uncool" or who are uncoordinated or fat or slow or "nerds"?

How would *Jesus* treat them? Is it possible that God might want us to be a glimpse of Jesus to someone who has "fallen through the cracks" today?

THE LIE TO REJECT

I reject the world's definition of "cool." I refuse to make fun of, treat coldly, or ignore the hurting, lonely, rejected people around me, for that is not the way of Jesus.

THE TRUTH TO ACCEPT

I accept the truth that God is so compassionate that He

sent Jesus to help the hurting people. I realize now that Jesus wants me to carry on that work in His name.

PRAYER FOR TODAY

Dear heavenly Father, forgive me for my cold, uncaring heart that turns away so often from those who need love. Please make me like Jesus. I want to be moved with compassion as He was and as You are. Open my eyes to the needs of people around me today and give me the love and courage to reach out to them. I'm afraid of what people will think of me if I do, but I know I must. I know You will always take care of me when I do Your will. In Jesus' compassionate name I pray. Amen.

READ ALL ABOUT IT

Mark 1

GOING DEEPER WITH GOD

Matthew 16

FROM BEGINNING TO END AND BEYOND

Lord, you have been our dwelling place throughout all generations. Before the mountains were born or you brought forth the earth and the world, from everlasting to everlasting you are God (Psalm 90:1,2 NIV).

Pick up a pen. Go ahead. I want you to think about something for a second. Got it? Okay.

Hold the pen in your hand. Twirl it around a little bit. Toss it up in the air. Catch it. Drop it. Pick it up again. Basically you can do whatever you want with that pen, right?

You can write truth or lies with it. Words of love or hate, beauty or profanity. You can write poetry or an encouraging letter or you can toss the pen into the trash or burn it in the fire.

For all intents and purposes, you control that pen.

Imagine for a moment that your pen represents *time*—all of the past, present, and future. One end represents the very beginning of all time and the other end represents the end of time—thousands upon thousands of years.

Imagine that the portion of the pen not covered by the cap represents past history, and the part covered by the cap represents the future. The lower edge of the cap is the present. Which is easier for you to see—the past, present, or future? The answer is obviously *all of the above!*

This simple exercise is designed to give you a picture of God that maybe you hadn't thought of before.

You see, Moses wrote in Psalm 90 that *"from everlasting to everlasting you are God"* (NIV). Simply put, God is eternal.

What does "eternal" mean? To try to understand that word, take a look at the pen again. The pen has a definite beginning and end. *Time* is like that. God started time rolling, and before that point time did not exist. In the future God will stop time, and after that point time will cease.

"Eternal" means time*less*, or apart from time. That's where God was, is, and always will be.

You see, there was not some point in time, way back, when God started to exist. Long before history began and before there was anything at all, there was God. He has always been there and always will be there.

He is there from the beginning to the end and beyond.

Think about that. Send your mind racing back in time. World War II. World War I. The Civil War. The Revolutionary War. The Pilgrims. The discovery of America. The Middle Ages. The Roman Empire. The time of Christ. The Greek, Persian, and Babylonian Empires. King David. Moses. Abraham. Noah and the flood. Adam and Eve. The Garden of Eden. The six days of creation. "In the beginning." Then nothing but God.

Send your mind sailing back as far as it can go. Through time. Before time. What will you find? As far as your mind can take you, there is God.

Are you dizzy yet? No? Good, 'cause we're just getting warmed up.

Shift from reverse into first gear, second gear, third gear and overdrive. Shoot your thoughts forward in time through the present and on into the future. To the next year. To the next century. To the return of Christ. To His thousand-year reign on earth. To the day of judgment. To the creation of the new heavens and new earth. To whatever comes next. What do you find? God again. He's already been there, done that!

God exists outside of time and so is not controlled by time, like we are. He, in fact, controls time. All of history—past, present, and future—is before God's eyes and in His hand all the time.

He knows the future as well as He knows the past. He knows what will be, won't be, could have been, and should have been.

He is like the author of a book, holding that book in his hand. The author knows what is on every page, because he wrote it. Even at the darkest moments in the story, the author knows how it will all turn out. He can easily flip to the last page and see that everything works out okay in the end.

Do you see how important it is to realize that God is eternal?

Moses wrote, "Lord, you have been our dwelling place throughout all generations" (NIV). It is the most natural thing in the world to make our safe, secure home in God once we know that all of history, including our life, is in His hands.

Are you worried about school? Graduation? A job? Making enough money to live on? A relationship? Getting married? Having a family? Losing a loved one? Sickness? Death?

Learn to trust God. He is not trapped in the present and ignorant of the future, like we are. He knows completely where we've come from, where we are and where we're going.

He sees our future successess and failures, joys and sorrows, victories and defeats. He sees the right way to go and the wrong way. He sees the obstacles and the pitfalls.

He sees the end from the beginning, because He is eternal.

"From everlasting to everlasting" He is God. He has never not been God and He always will be God. No one will ever be able to come along and take over His position as God. Isaiah, brilliantly inspired by God Himself, put it this way in chapter 43, verses 10-13 of his book:

> "You are My witnesses," declares the LORD. "And My servant whom I have chosen, in order that you may know and believe Me, and understand that I am He. Before Me there was no God formed, and there will be none after Me. I, even I, am the LORD; and there is no savior besides Me. It is I who have declared and saved and proclaimed, and there was no strange god among you. So you are My witnesses," declares the LORD, "And I am God. Even from eternity I am He, and there is none who can deliver out of My hand; I act and who can reverse it?"

Don't be alarmed if your head is swimming a little with the whole concept of God being eternal. Thinking about God is supposed to do that to us, at least a little bit. After all, He's God, and it shouldn't surprise us if there are things about Him that seem a bit mysterious.

Pick up that pen just one more time. Stare at it. If that pen represents all of time, how long would be your life measure on it? A fraction of a fraction of an inch, right?

Keep that in mind today as we conclude with more of of Moses' words from Psalm 90:

> You turn men back to dust, saying, "Return to dust, O sons of men." For a thousand years in your sight are like a day that has just gone by, or like a watch in the night. You sweep men away in the sleep of death; they are like the new grass of the morning— though in the morning it springs up new, by evening it is dry and withered.
>
> We are consumed by your anger and terrified by your indignation. You have set our iniquities before you, our secret sins in the light of your presence. All our days pass away under your wrath; we finish our years with a moan. The length of our days is seventy years—or eighty, if we have the strength; yet their span is but trouble and sorrow, for they quickly pass, and we fly away.
>
> Who knows the power of your anger? For your wrath is as great as the fear that is due you. Teach us to number our days aright, that we may gain a heart of wisdom (Psalm 90:3-12 NIV).

Read All About It

You already "read all about it" in Psalm 90!

Going Deeper with God

Matthew 17

ANYBODY THIRSTY?

*My people have committed two sins: They have for-
saken me, the spring of living water, and have dug their
own cisterns, broken cisterns that cannot hold water*
(Jeremiah 2:13 NIV).

It had been an unbearably hot summer all over western
Europe, and it was an unusually hot day for Switzerland.
The air was still and muggy and my friend and I were
sweating buckets while hiking through the foothills of the
Alps.

The scenery, though, was spectacular. From one spot we
had a panoramic view of snowcapped peaks wearing an
apron of lush, green meadows. I spotted two waterfalls cas-
cading down the sides of the mountains from the melting
snow above.

"Let's hike to one of those waterfalls!" I shouted enthu-
siastically to my friend. And off we went.

I walked as fast as I could through the sweltering afternoon heat, knowing that at the end of the hike was wonderful refreshment. It seemed like it was taking us forever
to reach the waterfall, but the roar of the falling water urged
us on. I knew it would be worth the work and the wait.

When we came through the woods and saw the waterfall, we just stood there in awe. Then I realized how hot I
was and so I ran to take a much-needed shower, but the
power of the falling water made it impossible to stand

directly under it. Still, I wanted to get as close to it as possible, so I yanked off my backpack and shirt and edged closer and closer.

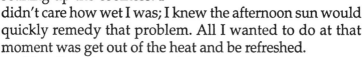

The contrast between the crisp, cold water crashing down and the hot air rising around the waterfall created a swirling wind that sent spray flying all around the base of the falls. I just stood in the spray, soaking up the coolness. I didn't care how wet I was; I knew the afternoon sun would quickly remedy that problem. All I wanted to do at that moment was get out of the heat and be refreshed.

King David wrote in Psalm 63:1 NIV:

> O God, you are my God, earnestly I seek you; my soul thirsts for you, my body longs for you in a dry and weary land where there is no water.

Our bodies get thirsty, and so do our souls. Our bodies crave water, and so do our souls.

The question is: When your soul is thirsty, where do you go to drink? In today's Scripture God pours out His grieving heart through the prophet Jeremiah. In essence, God is saying:

> The souls of My people are so thirsty. Their hearts are parched dry. But they have done two awful things. First they have forgotten that I am a flowing spring, a refreshing fountain of water, and so they have not come to Me. In fact, they have turned away from Me and dug wells in the ground to hold stagnant rainwater. But their wells are cracked and will not hold water at all.

What a tragedy when God's people seek refreshment everywhere but in God Himself, "the spring of living water"! Many of us, I'm afraid, have fallen into this trap. Somehow viewing God as boring or distant or mean, we try to fill the emptiness and fix the hurt inside with other things.

Popularity. Possessions. Performance (athletically, academically, artistically, etc.). Parties. Power.

Food. TV. Sex. Booze. Drugs. Music. The occult. Cults. Religious duty. Cynicism. Rebellion. Gangs. Crime.

You name it—just about anything can become a broken cistern if we let it. And not just bad things either. Good things and good people can become substitute gods when we run to them to fill the hollows in our heart, rather than running to God first.

Jesus was traveling one day through the region of Samaria. It was around noon and He was tired and thirsty, so He sat down by Jacob's well. Surprisingly, Jesus asked a Samaritan woman who was there to give Him a drink. The woman was amazed at this request, since Jews avoided Samaritans like the plague.

But Jesus was different. When He encountered a cultural law that violated God's law of love and liberty, He did the "unacceptable" without batting an eyelash. So He easily struck up a conversation with her.

The woman was intrigued by this man, and Jesus took the opportunity to stimulate her curiosity even more. He replied:

> If you knew the gift of God, and who it is who says to you, "Give Me a drink," you would have asked Him, and He would have given you living water (John 4:10).

The woman was clueless. She figured Jesus was still talking about the kind of water you drink. Patiently, Jesus opened her eyes to an even greater need in her life.

> Jesus answered and said to her, "Everyone who drinks of this water shall thirst again; but whoever drinks of the water that I shall give him shall never thirst; but the water that I shall give him shall become in him a well of water springing up to eternal life" (John 4:13,14).

By that time the woman was hooked. Whatever this man had, she wanted. But there was one problem, and Jesus knew what it was. She had dug out quite a few broken cisterns in her life and was working on another. Jesus exposed her sin gently but with crystal clarity:

> Jesus said to her, "You have well said, 'I have no husband'; for you have had five husbands; and the one whom you now have is not your husband; this you have said truly" (John 4:17,18).

The woman was stunned. Her life had just been exposed by this strange Jewish man, so she made the greatest understatement in the Bible:

> The woman said to Him, "Sir, I perceive that You are a prophet" (John 4:19).

After further conversation, she came to realize that Jesus was far more than just a prophet; he was the long-awaited Messiah. He was the Man that her thirsty soul had needed all her life.

She had gone through husbands like most people do cars, trading in the old one for a new and improved model. Five times.

Now finally she found what she had been looking a lifetime to find: not the fountain of youth, but the fountain of living waters. The Giver of eternal life. The only "drink" that can quench the soul's thirst.

The Messiah.

Is your soul thirsty today? You, too, have a choice. You can settle for stagnant rainwater, or you can stop by Jacob's well for a moment and ask for a drink of some *living* water from Jesus. The invitation still stands.

The Lie to Reject

I reject the lie that all my soul needs to be satisfied are things of this world. Although it is true that God will use things and people to meet my needs, I reject the lie that anyone or anything apart from God Himself can ultimately quench the thirst in my soul.

The Truth to Accept

I accept the truth that God alone is a spring of living water for my thirsty soul and that all my own efforts to meet the deepest needs in my life are like broken cisterns that can hold no water.

Prayer for Today

Dear heavenly Father, I confess to You that I usually do not see You as the fountain and spring of living waters that You are. Many times I have not really believed that You had what it takes to fill up the empty places in my life. I thank You for Your generosity in giving so many

wonderful gifts in this world—both people and things.
May those gifts be a reminder to me of You and may they
draw me to You as the source of life. I choose today to pause
and drink deeply from Your presence. May the richness
and fullness of You in my soul overflow to refresh others
around me today. In Jesus' name. Amen.

READ ALL ABOUT IT

John 4

GOING DEEPER WITH GOD

Matthew 18

THE GOD WHO HEALS

*When evening had come, they brought to Him many
who were demon-possessed; and He cast out the spirits
with a word, and healed all who were ill in order that
what was spoken through Isaiah the prophet might be
fulfilled, saying, "He Himself took our infirmities, and
carried away our diseases"* (Matthew 8:16,17).

When you read in the Bible about the life of Jesus, perhaps nothing stands out more than the miracles He did: healing the blind, the deaf, the sick, the lame—even raising the dead. Page after page explodes with marvelous stories of God's healing power unleashed through Jesus Christ.

Do you ever wonder if God still heals today? May the following stories remove all doubt from your mind.

In Rara, Ghana, a crowd of 3,000 was gathered to watch the *Jesus* film.[1]

Less than halfway through the two-hour film, a woman in the crowd started shouting and crying, "My baby is dying! My baby is dying!" Her ten-month-old baby girl had gone completely stiff in her arms.

Immediately the leader of the film team stopped the film, and, joined by a few other believers, rushed over to the woman. They took the child from her arms and began praying, "O God, You have healed the humpbacked lady. You have healed the blind man. You have raised the daughter of Jairus from the dead. You can heal this baby. Show Your mighty power. Heal this little baby to show Your love, and for Your glory." [2]

The curious crowd had just watched actors on the film portray Jesus' healing ministry. Suddenly they saw "live" what Jesus can do as the baby went limp in the leader's arms and began to cry!

The film leader turned to the crowd and cried out, "What Jesus did on the film, He has done for this little baby girl! Jesus is the most powerful, most loving God in the universe. He can heal you, He can forgive your sins, and He can make it possible for You to live forever with Him." [3]

The entire crowd came forward to put their faith in Jesus . . . all 3000 of them! [4] A woman in despair received new hope and a crowd of needy people in a dusty village in Africa received new life.

In Thailand the *Jesus* film was being shown one night in a schoolyard. The film team rigged up a loudspeaker and broadcast the film through it so that people all over the village could listen to the movie.

A hundred yards or so from the film showing, a lame man lay sick in bed in his house. As he listened to the *Jesus* film, he learned that Jesus could heal the sick, so he wondered if He could do that for him.

Because of a crippled leg he could not walk, but he pushed himself up onto his hands and knees and prayed, "Jesus, if You are the living and true God and have power to heal sickness, I pray that You heal me now." [5]

The man immediately got up, ran outside, and rushed over to the team leader, explaining what Jesus had done for him. He was so excited he wanted to pay the leader five dollars.

The money was politely turned down, but the healed man insisted he stay with him that night. In the morning he gathered his entire family together to hear how they could become Christians! [6]

The *Jesus* film is the Gospel of Luke on film. Translated into well over 300 languages, it has been shown in at least 216 countries to over 700 million people around the world. One of the scenes in the film depicts this moving story from Luke 7:

> It came about soon afterward that He went to a city called Nain; and His disciples were going along with Him, accompanied by a large multitude. Now as He approached the gate of the city, behold, a dead man was being carried out, the only son of his mother, and she was a widow; and a sizeable crowd from the city was with her. And when the Lord saw her, He felt compassion for her, and said to her, "Do not weep."
>
> And He came up and touched the coffin; and the bearers came to a halt. And He said, "Young man, I say to you, arise!" And the dead man sat up, and began to speak. And Jesus gave him back to his mother. And fear gripped them all, and they began glorifying God, saying, "A great prophet has arisen among us!" and "God has visited His people!" (Luke 7:11-16).

What can we learn from these three stories? That God has indeed visited His people and continues to do so today, moving with His powerful healing hand. Jesus healed people when He was here on earth because He was filled with compassion, and He still heals people today because He hasn't changed one bit. He still feels the pain of people and is moved to act.

Does God heal everyone? No, at least not here on earth. Why He chooses to heal one but not another is a mystery we do not and probably cannot understand.

We dare not put God in a box. There are some who would put God in a box by denying that He heals at all today in a supernatural way. That is a box in which God simply will not stay! He blows that one apart every day all over the world.

There are others who would put God in a box that says God always desires to completely heal here on earth. Those who are not cured are then dismissed as "not having enough faith."

How many people have remained ill or even died while wracked with the cruel (and false!) guilt that torments them with the accusation *If you only had more faith.*

The compassionate, caring Jesus never demands that we have the level of faith that says, *Lord, I know You will.* He only asks that we be able to say, *Lord, I know You can.*

For those who are asked to wait until heaven for their healing, the apostle Paul has words of encouragement. He knows what it means to wait. Paul asked God three times to remove some affliction from his body but God said no . . . three times. But God also said:

> My grace is sufficient for you, for My power is perfected in weakness (2 Corinthians 12:9).

The God who heals does not always do so in the way or at the time we would like Him to. Life is simply not as clear cut as we would like it to be.

But Paul learned that God's grace is enough for now. God promised that it would be.

THE LIE TO REJECT

I reject the lie that God never heals supernaturally anymore. I refuse to put God in that box. In addition, I reject

*the lie that it is always God's design to heal us completely
on earth.*

The Truth to Accept

*I accept the fact that God is merciful and compassionate
but I also realize that His ways are higher than ours. I
choose to believe that He can choose whom He heals on
earth and whom He will heal in heaven.*

Prayer for Today

*Dear heavenly Father, You are the God who heals. Your
Word shows that to be true and eyewitness accounts con-
firm that as well. I thank You that You do not change. The
same compassion that moved the Lord Jesus to heal while
He was on earth still moves Him today. But, Lord, sometimes it's hard to keep on trusting You when people I know
and love are not healed. Why is that? I really want to know,
but I accept the reality that I won't know the answer to
that question until I see You in heaven. I know that Your
ways will make perfect sense to me then. Until that time
I choose to trust You. In the name of Jesus my healer. Amen.*

Read All About It

Luke 7

Going Deeper with God

Matthew 19

JOIN UP! JOIN IN!

*Remember the former things long past, for I am God,
and there is no other; I am God, and there is no one like
Me, declaring the end from the beginning and from
ancient times things which have not been done, saying,
"My purpose will be established, and I will accomplish all My good pleasure"* (Isaiah 46:9,10).

Is God really in control of what happens on this planet?
Does He know what He's doing? Does He have any kind of
plan, or do things just kind of happen?

Today's Scripture tells us that God does indeed have a
plan and that His purposes will be established. Life is not
just some sort of confused chaos of chance happenings. God
is in control and He is right on schedule to do what He wants
to do. Some people doubt that He is really there and in
charge, but the Bible says that without a shadow of a doubt
God *is* in control:

Why should the nations say, "Where, now, is their
God?" But our God is in the heavens; He does whatever He pleases (Psalm 115:2,3).

Job learned the truth the hard way that God is in charge.
After his suffering had ended and God had blessed and pros-
pered him again, he said:

I know that you can do all things; no plan of yours
can be thwarted (Job 42:2 NIV).

Although some of what God is up to remains a mystery, He also chooses to reveal "the end from the beginning" to us. These glimpses of the future are called prophecies and those who make them are called prophets. Many of the writers of the Bible included prophecies of future events in their books. The Old Testament, for example, is filled with hundreds of predictions about the Messiah, Jesus Christ.

God did not want us to miss Him when He came, so He laid out a road map to find Him. The following chart is designed to give you just a taste of the prophecies made about Jesus, so you can see how wonderfully God is in control.

As you look at these predictions, made hundreds of years before Jesus' birth, may the Lord fill you with awe. God's plans came to pass, just as He said they would! And even the strongest efforts of evil men and the devil could not and cannot stop Him. In fact, their wicked ways were (and are) simply used by God to accomplish His purposes. There is no doubt about it, God is calling the shots!

Some Prophecies of Jesus

Prophecy	Old Testament Prediction	New Testament Fulfillment
Born in Bethlehem	Micah 5:2	Matthew 2:1
Born of a virgin	Isaiah 7:14	Matthew 1:22,23
Sinless	Isaiah 53:9	1 Peter 2:21-23
Mocked	Psalm 22:6-8	Luke 23:35-39
Cast lots for clothes	Psalm 22:18	John 19:23,24
Died for sins	Isaiah 53:5,6	1 Peter 3:18
Buried in rich man's tomb	Isaiah 53:9	Mark 15:42-47
Resurrected	Psalm 16:9,10	Matthew 28:1-10

Take a few minutes and look up these prophecies. You'll be amazed! We'll use this exercise as a substitute for the usual **Read All About It** section.

If someone's heart is not set against Jesus already, the few prophecies listed above would be enough to convince them that He is the Messiah. And we are just scratching the surface with these; there are many, many more!

One amazing prediction is found in Zechariah 11:12,13 and concerns details of how the Messiah would be betrayed:

> I said to them, "If it is good in your sight, give me my wages; but if not, never mind!" So they weighed out thirty shekels of silver as my wages. Then the LORD said to me, "Throw it to the potter, that magnificent price at which I was valued by them." So I took the thirty shekels of silver and threw them to the potter in the house of the LORD.

Zechariah prophesied those words about 500 years before the time of Jesus' betrayal by Judas. Compare what he wrote with the historical account recorded by Matthew:

> Then one of the Twelve—the one called Judas Iscariot—went to the chief priests and asked, "What are you willing to give me if I hand him over to you?" So they counted out for him thirty silver coins...
>
> When Judas, who had betrayed him, saw that Jesus was condemned, he was seized with remorse and returned the thirty silver coins to the chief priests and the elders. "I have sinned," he said, "for I have betrayed innocent blood."
>
> "What is that to us?" they replied. "That's your responsibility." So Judas threw the money into the

> temple and left. Then he went away and hanged himself.
>
> The chief priests picked up the coins and said, "It is against the law to put this into the treasury, since it is blood money." So they decided to use the money to buy the potter's field as a burial place for foreigners (Matthew 26:14,15; 27:3-7 NIV).

Can you believe the detail of Zechariah's prediction? How could He have been so specific and so right 500 years before an event took place?

Because God is in control. He knows the end from the beginning, down to the most minute detail. He could have had Zechariah predict exactly how many of the 30 coins would have landed "heads" and which would have landed "tails." God could have told us the exact time of day it all happened, and what color clothes everyone wore and what they had eaten for lunch that day and....

Are you getting the picture? When it comes to the events of history, we can say with complete confidence, "I know that the LORD is great, that our Lord is greater than all gods. The LORD does whatever pleases him, in the heavens and on the earth" (Psalm 135:5,6 NIV). God is in control.

Does this mean that everything that happens is God's perfect will? Of course not. Every time we sin we go against His will. And that happens billions of times a day around the world!

What the verse means is that God has His purposes for the world and they *will* come to pass. Christ came once and He will come again. That's a done deal. Those who believe in Him will be escorted to their eternal honeymoon cottage in heaven and those who reject Him will suffer eternally. You can count on it.

God also has His purposes for your life and mine. Mainly, He desires to make us like His Son, Jesus (Romans 8:29), and involve us in His work of building the kingdom of God (Matthew 16:18).

Will you cooperate with God's incredible plans to make you all that you were created to be? Will you join Him in His marvelous work of bringing a lost and dying world back to Himself?

In the end, God will fulfill His plans with or without us. He doesn't *need* us. But He *wants* us. Why not make the decision today? Join up and join in!

The Lie to Reject

I reject the lie that life is out of control, with no purpose or meaning to it. I refuse to focus on my circumstances or feelings that tell me God is not in control, or that His will is not good for me.

The Truth to Accept

I accept the truth that God is accomplishing His purposes in the world and that He is right on time. I choose to believe that His purposes for me are good, acceptable, and perfect (Romans 12:2).

Prayer for Today

Dear Lord, what a relief to know that You are in charge. When all is said and done, the world will know that You were, are, and always will be the King. Your ultimate purposes cannot be stopped, not even by the most wicked men or angels. Lord, Your Word says that You want to make me like Jesus, so that He can shine through me to a dark world. I can't imagine a greater purpose or meaning to my life than that. So I choose today to give up all of my smaller purposes, goals, dreams, and ambitions and lay them before Your grand purpose. If You choose to fulfill my dreams, because they are a part of Your dream for me, then fine. If not, I'll know that Your plans are better. In Jesus' name. Amen.

GOING DEEPER WITH GOD

Matthew 20

A BIG, BIG HEART

Jesus came up and spoke to them, saying, "All authority has been given to Me in heaven and on earth. Go therefore and make disciples of all the nations . . . and lo, I am with you always, even to the end of the age " (Matthew 28:18-20).

My wife, Shirley, and I had been married about three months when the letter came.

She had grown up, gone to school, and served the Lord in the South all her life. And then she married a Yankee and was living just outside of Philadelphia. She had her hands full with cultural adjustments, to say the least.

In addition, we didn't start out too well financially in our marriage, so there was the added stress of having to cut corners on a new budget. We also had to trust God to raise additional financial support to make up for what had dropped off.

As if that weren't enough (and I guess God didn't think it was!), Shirley and I were exchanging germs. I'd get sick and she'd be well. Then I'd get better and she'd catch whatever I had. Then we'd repeat the process over again. This went on for months.

Then the letter came.

My first reaction was to sneeze (I was sick), then laugh and then get mad. Shirley's response was to cry.

I remember her moaning, "I've just got my drapes up!"

The letter had asked us to pray about moving to the Philippines to direct a new high school ministry in Metro Manila. The leadership of our ministry was not telling us we had to go, although they felt it was a very good fit for us.

"Thanks a lot," I grumbled. "That's easy for them to say. They're probably thinking, 'Here am I, Lord, send the Millers!'" I was not in a good mood.

To understand why I reacted so negatively, you have to realize I had been to the Philippines in the summer of 1980, showing the *Jesus* film. It had been an incredible two months of ministry, but to be honest, I had had my fill of the tropics.

My body is designed more for Siberia than Singapore. I start to get comfortable when the temperature outside drops below 50 degrees. On a "cool" day in Manila, the afternoon temperature might dip to a frigid 85 degrees!

And then there's the humidity. In the Philippines, the relative humidity is at least as high as the temperature, taking it off the charts in the "Miller Discomfort Index."

So I tossed the letter in the trash and tried not to think about it.

Sure I had told the Lord I would go anywhere in the world and do anything He wanted, but I felt like I'd already paid my dues in the Sweat Capital of the World. I was waiting for a call to Switzerland or some place like that.

In fact, one summer I had traveled to Switzerland and loved it so much I told a missionary I met, "You know, I think God might be calling me back here." He chuckled and told me, "Everybody thinks they hear the voice of God when they come to Switzerland. It's really just your own voice echoing off the mountains!"

For several months I tried to put the idea of moving to the Philippines out of my head, but it wouldn't leave. Much to my dismay, when I'd ask Shirley what she was thinking about the move, she'd get excited.

"Well, it *is* a great opportunity," she would say.

She was right about that. The Filipinos are some of the most receptive people to the gospel in the entire world. And the commitment was for only two to three years.

"Two to three years of sweating," I sighed to myself. I still wasn't convinced I should go.

One day while I was praying I had a vision of sorts. I pictured myself standing before the Lord one day.

"So, Rich, why did you never go to the Philippines?" The Lord was looking me straight in the eye.

I shuffled uncomfortably, looking down. "Well, Lord, You know how I hate the heat and the humidity. Besides, I've already been there. Can't you send somebody else? I feel called to help bring revival to America anyway."

In my mind I had this strange feeling that God was not pleased with my answer. Somehow I didn't think He would accept my not going simply because I don't like to sweat.

So I said, "All right, Lord, You win. If You really want me to go, I'm willing. Please show me from Your Word."

Does the word "immediately" mean anything to you? It did to me at that moment, because He immediately impressed it on my mind to turn to Matthew 28:18-20 (today's Scripture).

I already knew what it said, but when I read it again the word "Go" hit me so hard I almost started packing my bags right then and there.

"Okay, Lord," I said glumly, "I'm going to move toward going, because Your Word says 'Go.' If I'm not supposed to go for some reason, You're going to have to stop me."

The final words of the book of Matthew suddenly were more comforting than ever before: "Lo, I am with you always, even to the end of the age." I knew that without His precious presence there was no way we could leave family, friends, and the familiar sights and sounds of America.

About four months later, after selling two cars, putting all our stuff in storage, and saying tearful goodbyes to loved ones, we were gone. Walking onto that plane was one of the toughest things I've ever done. I was so thankful to have a wife who loved Jesus sitting next to me as we flew west.

Twenty-seven months later we were flying home again. Our family had grown, and so had our hearts.

When we took off from Ninoy Aquino International Airport in Manila, we left behind some of the dearest friends and colaborers in the ministry we'll probably ever have. And we left a ministry that had an impact on over 100,000 young people in Metro Manila and beyond!

I can't wait to get to heaven to see all that God did in and through the lives of those teenagers we were privileged to touch.

God has a heart as big as (and bigger!) than the world, and I'm glad Shirley and I had the chance to watch His love in action.

Was it easy? No. In addition to the sweltering heat and humidity, there were constant power outages, monumental traffic jams, smells like you would not believe, hideous smog, and (my wife's favorite) roaches so big they could eat your children if you didn't watch out!

I also suffered from a serious bout with pneumonia which resulted in a dangerous asthma condition.

Are we glad we went? You betcha. And, to be honest, we're glad we're back, too!

And the Lord has given us the opportunity now to see revival come to the lives of youth and young adults in

America, just like we dreamed. But before He could give us that kind of ministry here, He had some major surgery to do on our hearts. And His operating table just happened to be in the Philippines.

THE LIE TO REJECT

I reject the lie that giving up comfort and leisure for the cause of Christ is an unhealthy or unnecessary sacrifice. I refuse to selfishly pursue my own pleasure while many around me and millions around the world are dying without Christ.

THE TRUTH TO ACCEPT

I accept the truth that God's big heart is beating for people from every tribe, tongue, people, and nation. I choose therefore to accept my calling as an ambassador for Christ to go and do whatever my Lord asks of me.

PRAYER FOR TODAY

Dear heavenly Father, I have had "tunnel vision" when it comes to what's on Your heart. My field of vision has been limited mainly to my own needs and those of a few friends and family. Help me to lift up my eyes and see the fields of the world, that they are ripe for harvest. Please show me how I can be more a part of what You are doing to see the gospel go to the ends of the earth. How shall I pray? What shall I give? Do you want me to go, either on a short-term or long-term mission? You are the Lord of the harvest. I ask You to send laborers into the harvest field, and I stand here today, Lord, and pray, "Here am I; send me." In the authority of the name of Jesus, I pray. Amen.

Read All About It

Acts 1

Going Deeper with God

Matthew 21

GO IN PEACE

He said to the woman, "Your faith has saved you; go in peace" (Luke 7:50).

Sinner. Prostitute. Whore. She wore her label like a scarlet letter. Everybody knew her and everybody knew what kind of life she led.

Some snickered when they saw her approach, others whispered behind her back, others pulled out their wallets. But they all despised her.

She was handy to have around whenever people started feeling a little guilty for their sin. "Well, at least I'm not as bad as that prostitute," they could always say, and then they'd feel better about themselves.

The religious leaders of the day, the Pharisees, would not be caught dead near her—at least not in broad daylight, and certainly not during a meal. That was simply not kosher.

And that's why it must have been such a shock to see her walk in on a private meal at Simon the Pharisee's house. Here's the story put in my own words, apologies to Dr. Luke:

> One of the religious honchos, a Pharisee named Simon, invited Jesus over to his house for a meal, and Jesus accepted the invitation.

> Things were going along pretty much as expected—Simon checking out Jesus and Jesus reading Simon like a book, when a Pharisee's worst nightmare happened.

You see, there happened to be a particular street walker, a lady of the evening, in town who heard on the street that Jesus was eating over at Simon's place. So she grabbed a small bottle of expensive perfume that she had purchased with her... uh... salary, and normally wore when she was... er... working and took off for Simon's house.

Simon nearly choked on his bagels and lox when she walked in.

That was bad enough, but then, to him at least, things began to get really ugly. She didn't just say "Hi" to Jesus and then "hasta luego." Oh no, she hung around, behind Jesus. Then she started to cry, dripping her disgusting tears all over Jesus' feet.

Then Simon simply had to turn away. It was too much for any good Jew to take. She dried her tears from His feet and started kissing them! And she just kept on and on and on.

And if that weren't enough, then came the perfume. She poured that expensive fragrance all over Jesus' feet. What a waste! The whole stinking house started to smell of it.

Simon couldn't believe the scene taking place in front of him. But there was one silver lining in this dark cloud of a meal. It confirmed to Simon what he had already hoped were true. This Jesus guy was a fraud.

He muttered under his breath, "If this dude Jesus were anything special, he'd know what sort of human sewage this woman is. It's obvious he's no prophet. I knew it all along."

Jesus answered Simon as if the Pharisee had been talking out loud rather than to himself.

"Simon, I'd like to have a word with you."

"Go ahead, Teacher, shoot."

So Jesus shot. "Have you heard the story about the two guys who went into a bank to get a loan? One borrowed about 50,000 bucks and the other borrowed about 5000. But neither of them could pay off the loan.

"Unbelievably, the bank manager just decided to forget about the whole thing and canceled both debts. Which of the two guys who owed the bank money will love the bank manager more? Take a wild guess."

Rolling his eyes a bit and yawning, Simon replied, "I suppose it would have to be the one who was forgiven the 50,000-dollar debt."

"Simon says correctly," Jesus responded.

Jesus then turned around and smiled at the woman who was still standing behind Him. "Simon, do you see this woman? I know you do, even though you're trying to ignore her. When I came over for this meal, my feet were dusty and it is customary to have your guest's feet washed. But you didn't lift a finger to do that. But this woman has washed my feet with her tears and dried them with her hair.

"Furthermore, when I entered your house, you did not give me the polite greeting of a kiss on the cheek, but ever since I set foot in this place, this woman has been kissing my feet.

"Nor did you pour oil on My head as a greeting, but she has anointed My feet with this perfume."

By this time the woman's eyes were as big as saucers. Jesus had accepted her love! It was the first time a man had ever loved her for anything except.... Her heart was about to burst with joy.

On the other hand, Simon's eyes grew narrower and narrower with rage. He felt like ending the meal and shooing this man out of his house like a pesky fly. But common courtesy would not permit that, and neither somehow would Jesus.

"Simon, here's the point: This woman who we all agree has sinned terribly in her life has been forgiven of all those sins, because she loved greatly. But the one who has been forgiven little loves little."

Turning again to the woman, He said, "Your sins have all been forgiven."

Shocked, Simon and the others at the table whispered to each other, "Who does he think he is, forgiving people's sins! Why, the nerve of the man!"

Ignoring them, Jesus smiled again at the woman and said, "Your faith has saved you. Now go in peace" (Adapted from Luke 7:36-50).

Maybe you feel like that woman today. You've done so many things you're ashamed of—some things no one knows but you, other things everybody seems to know and nobody wants to forget.

You've confessed your sins a million times but your past haunts you like a ghost that will not leave. You wonder what Jesus *really* thinks of you.

Listen to His words and take heart: "Your sins have been forgiven." Take heart. "Your faith has saved you; go in peace."

Thℇ Lℇ to Rℇjℇct

I reject the lie that my sin is too great for Jesus to forgive. I will not give in to the devil's accusations that I have sinned too often or too terribly for Him to cleanse me.

THE TRUTH TO ACCEPT

I joyfully accept the truth that God's grace is greater than my sin. My faith in Christ has saved me and I may go in peace, knowing God's complete forgiveness and cleansing from my sin.

PRAYER FOR TODAY

Lord, I must admit that at times in my life I have felt like and acted like both the woman in the story as well as Simon the Pharisee. Sometimes I have felt so dirty that I wondered if You could or would ever smile at me again. And then when I came to You in repentance, You did! Every time, no matter how many times I came, you forgave me. But other times, when I felt I was doing well spiritually, I looked down on others who were struggling. I compared myself to them and felt proud, rather than comparing myself to You and being humbled. In Your eyes, I believe these times were worse than the other. I thank You that I can indeed go in peace because of the finished work of Christ on the cross. In Jesus' name. Amen.

READ ALL ABOUT IT

Mark 14 (learn something interesting about Simon!)

GOING DEEPER WITH GOD

Matthew 22

THE DEVIL'S WORST NIGHTMARE

Having disarmed the powers and authorities, he made a public spectacle of them, triumphing over them by the cross (Colossians 2:15 NIV).

The SWAT team—Special Weapons And Tactics. Every large city has one. They're a group of highly skilled, superbly trained police officers loaded to the gills with the firepower to get the job done.

They're not called in to do ordinary, everyday police stuff. You don't waste their time directing traffic outside a stadium parking lot. You don't send them out on the interstate to man a speed trap. Their purpose is to handle the toughest, most dangerous assignments.

Like hostage rescue.

Brent Braunworth knows what he's talking about. He's a medic on a SWAT team in West Palm Beach, Florida.

"A SWAT team's best friend is the element of surprise. Within seconds we appear out of nowhere, guns aimed, moving so quickly and efficiently that suspects don't know what's going on."[1]

He got an "up close and personal" view of that efficiency when his unit was called in to rescue a woman whose drug-using boyfriend was holding her hostage.

The unit quickly but cautiously approached the second-floor dwelling, moving "quietly along the concrete walkway, keeping low, crawling under windows to get on either side of the apartment."[2]

They crouched silently outside the suspect's door, the tension mounting. The "nest" of snipers was in place across the street while the police negotiator talked to the suspect on the phone, trying to bring a peaceful end to the whole thing. He could come out any moment. Would he have the hostage with him? Here's what happened, as told by Brent:

> Minutes pass. I reposition my handgun in my fingers. Not a sound can be heard. We are in doorways, around corners and under windows, either kneeling or on our bellies.
>
> The door cracks, then slowly opens outward. Light from the apartment falls on the walkway, and we push backward into the darkness. The suspect has the woman with him; the knife is at her throat.
>
> As he looks down the walkway, we pounce. Our first man comes from behind the door, grabbing the knife. Another separates the woman from him and ties up his other hand. The rest of us swarm on him like mosquitoes at dusk. In less than a minute he is subdued and cuffed. [3]

The woman ran back inside the apartment, where Brent found her. She was nervous and crying, but she was unhurt. And she was free.[4]

The human race was in a desperate hostage situation. Satan, the "god of this world," had the entire world in captivity, with a knife at its throat.

So Jesus, a one-man SWAT team, decided to take action. The writer of Hebrews put it this way:

> Since then the children share in flesh and blood, He Himself likewise also partook of the same, that

through death He might render powerless him who had the power of death, that is, the devil, and might deliver those who through fear of death were subject to slavery all their lives (Hebrews 2:14,15).

Jesus subdued the devil. He rendered him powerless. Satan no longer holds the children of God hostage. Jesus rescued us single-handedly and delivered us from the bondage of sin and the fear of death.

What were Jesus' "special weapons and tactics"? He chose a weapon that the devil came up with himself. In fact, he handed it to Jesus. He even made sure people like Judas Iscariot, Herod, Caiaphas (the high priest), and Pontius Pilate carried out his plan.

The weapon that was used to destroy the devil's work (1 John 3:8) was death! The death of Jesus.

What? How could the death of the hero be called a victory? Most people (including the disciples) thought it was the end of Jesus. And so did the devil.

Remember what Brent said was the SWAT team's "best friend"? That's right, the element of surprise.

Satan was caught completely off guard. When Jesus died on the cross He cried out, "It is finished!" (John 19:30). I can just picture the devil scratching his head. He was probably expecting something more like "I am finished!" from the mouth of Jesus.

Little did Satan know that when Jesus died on the cross He—

1. paid the penalty of death for the sins of the world;

2. provided freedom from the bondage of sin to all who would believe in Him;

3. opened the door to eternal life and freedom from death;

4. defeated the devil by taking away his power to keep believers under the control of sin and death.

But it all became perfectly clear to Satan three days later when Jesus exploded from the tomb, breaking the chains of death on that first Easter Sunday.

It was the devil's worst nightmare come true. He who was the master of trickery and deception was caught in the greatest "sting operation" ever performed.

When Jesus rose from the grave, He moved in with lightning speed, yanked the weapons from the devil's hands, and set the hostage free. Then he cuffed Satan and paraded him in front of the entire world of angels as the defeated, humiliated enemy he is.

"A public spectacle" is how Paul described it in Colossians 2:15. The picture is of a conquering Roman hero:

> When a general defeated the opposing forces and won the battle, a "triumphal procession" would occur to celebrate the victory. The successful general would lead the procession, followed by his army singing hymns of victory and jubilantly reveling in their conquest. Also in the parade would be the defeated king along with all his surviving warriors. The disheartened and subdued enemies became a public spectacle for ridicule, with their subjugation paraded for all to see. In a similar fashion, God has thus put the principalities and powers [Satan and the demons] on public display, revealing their powerlessness before Christ. [5]

Who is the conquering general? The Lord Jesus Christ! Who is His army "singing hymns of victory and jubilantly reveling in their conquest"? We are!

The devil's worst nightmare has become a dream come true for us. Satan has been defeated and we are free! Praise the Lord!

The Lie to Reject

I reject the lie that I am unable to stand against the devil's powerful schemes. I refuse to believe his lies that would make him look like the victor and make me look like the defeated one.

The Truth to Accept

I proclaim the truth that Satan is a defeated, disarmed and humiliated foe and that I am in Jesus Christ, the Victor. Therefore I affirm today that in Christ I have the strength and power I need to resist the devil and flee from temptation and sin.

Prayer for Today

Most victorious Lord, I praise You and worship You. You have triumphed over sin, death, and the devil through Christ's death, resurrection, and ascension to Your right hand in heaven. No matter what my feelings may say or what my circumstances might tell me, Your victory and the devil's defeat are real. By faith, today I choose to enter into Your victory parade, singing songs of praise to You and keeping my eyes to the front. Help me to keep my eyes fixed on Jesus this day, remembering that He is the glorious, victorious King. In His name, which is above every name, I pray. Amen.

READ ALL ABOUT IT
Colossians 2

GOING DEEPER WITH GOD
Matthew 23

IT'S A SMALL WORLD AFTER ALL

O LORD, our Lord, how majestic is Thy name in all the earth! (Psalm 8:9).

"The universe *has* to be millions of years old," the class atheist said matter-of-factly after I finished my classroom talk on "Creation Versus Evolution." "You see, stars are millions of light years away and so it has taken millions of years for the light from those stars to just reach our eyes so we could even see them!" He waited for my response.

"But what if God created them so that people on earth could see them right away? After all, if God created stars to show us how awesome and powerful He is, why wait millions of years for us to see the first one? That doesn't make much sense to me."

What that atheistic student had said was perfectly logical and made good science sense—if you leave God out of your system of thought.

Genesis 1:1 starts out by saying:

> In the beginning God created the heavens and the earth.

That pretty much sums it up. The universe is not eternal; it once was not but now it is. It did not come to the place it is now by mere chance plus time, either. God created it. If you want to believe He created it with a big bang, go ahead. At that moment the only ears to hear the bang would have been God's (and possibly angels') ears anyway!

If you live in the city, what I'm going to ask you to do will be hard. So put it on your "to do" list the next time you venture out into the country, or even better, the wilderness.

If you live far away from city or suburban lights, you've no doubt done this many times already: On a warm, clear night, lie on your back outside and look at the stars.

What you will feel at that moment (especially if it is quiet outside) is a healthy sense of awe. It may begin to dawn on you that our planet, for all the noise and activity that goes on here, is just a small speck in the universe. And when you realize that the God of the universe can hold the whole thing in the "palm of His hand," another important truth may dawn on you as well: God is *big!*

The prophet Isaiah, wanting to encourage the Jewish nation to trust God, wrote:

> "To whom then will you liken Me, that I should be his equal?" says the Holy One. "Lift up your eyes on high and see who has created these stars, the One who leads forth their host by number; He calls them all by name; because of the greatness of His might and the strength of His power not one of them is missing" (Isaiah 40:25,26).

Billions and billions of stars in billions and billions of galaxies (Can't you just hear Carl Sagan saying that?) and God knows them all by name! Red giants. Supernovas. Dwarfs. Whatever is out there, God calls it by name. "Come here, George!" I wonder what name He has for our sun. Something a lot more creative than "sun," I bet!

Now I don't know about you, but I have trouble remembering all the names of people in my church. And God remembers billions of names of stars? What an incredible mind our God has!

Somewhere out in a Middle Eastern desert, centuries ago and on a clear, warm night, that shepherd boy turned king, David, stretched out under heaven's roof and looked up. What he saw was so awesome that he wrote a song about it. And God placed it in His favorite hymnbook for people like us to enjoy.

> O Lord, our Lord, how majestic is your name in all the earth! You have set your glory above the heavens. From the lips of children and infants you have ordained praise because of your enemies, to silence the foe and the avenger.
>
> When I consider your heavens, the work of your fingers, the moon and the stars, which you have set in place, what is man that you are mindful of him, the son of man that you care for him?
>
> You made him a little lower than the heavenly beings and crowned him with glory and honor.
>
> You made him ruler over the works of your hands; you put everything under his feet: all flocks and herds, and the beasts of the field, the birds of the air, and the fish of the sea, all that swim the paths of the seas.
>
> O LORD, our Lord, how majestic is your name in all the earth! (Psalm 8 NIV).

When you look up at the stars, you can't help but wonder, "Why does God bother with us here on earth at all? We are such a small dot on the universe's map."

But when you look in the Word of God you see something else, something amazing: You see a God who has bent down and crowned mankind with glory and honor and given him planet Earth to rule over.

Mankind. *Small* by the universe's standards but *significant* by God's. *Humble* when compared to the vastness of creation and the even greater vastness of the Creator, but *honored* by that same God.

As you think about those things, whether inside lying on your bed or outside lying in a meadow in the middle of nowhere, may they lead you to the same conclusion David made thousands of years ago:

> O LORD, our Lord, how majestic is Your name in all the earth!

THE LIE TO REJECT

I reject the lie that the universe as a whole and man in particular got here by the chance plus time equation of evolution. I refuse to buy into the devil's lie that the human race is no more significant than the animal kingdom, and that life itself is basically meaningless.

THE TRUTH TO ACCEPT

I accept the truth that a majestic and loving Creator created the heavens and the earth and that I am a significant part of that creation. I believe my life is meaningful because I am created in the image of God and united for eternity with Jesus Christ.

PRAYER FOR TODAY

Most loving and awesome God, Creator and Sustainer of the whole universe, how majestic is Your name in all the earth! When I look at the vastness, creativity, and beauty of Your creation I stand in awe of You. And to think that You, Lord, have saved me and adopted me into Your family and given me a life of meaning, purpose, and significance in Christ just blows me away! Thinking about the size of the universe and the multitude of stars humbles me, Lord, and reminds me that if You are big enough to control the huge expanse of outer space, You are certainly able to take care of me. I trust You today and every day to do just that. In Jesus' name. Amen.

READ ALL ABOUT IT

Job 38

GOING DEEPER WITH GOD

Matthew 24

The God Who Serves

For who is greater, the one who reclines at table, or the one who serves? Is it not the one who reclines at table? But I am among you as the one who serves (Luke 22:27).

Dr. Paul Brand has invested a lifetime serving. As a world-renowned hand surgeon and leprosy specialist, he lived among the lepers of India ministering healing to suffering bodies and souls.

In his eye-opening book *Pain: The Gift Nobody Wants* he tells about a remarkable man who was known simply as "Uncle Robbie."

> I have met a few "living saints" in my time, men and women who at great personal pains and sacrifice have devoted themselves to the care of others.
>
> As I have watched these rare individuals in action, though, any thought of personal sacrifice fades away. I find myself envying, not pitying them. In the process of giving away life, they find it and achieve a level of contentment and peace virtually unknown to the rest of the world.
>
> I think of a man we all called "Uncle Robbie," a New Zealander who turned up at Vellore [a city in India] one day, unannounced. "I have a little experience in shoe-making," he said; "I wonder if I could be of help to your leprosy patients. I'm retired now, and don't need money. Just a bench and a few tools."

The facts of Uncle Robbie's life leaked out slowly. We were amazed to learn that he had been an orthopedic surgeon—had, in fact, been chief of all orthopedics in New Zealand. He had given up surgery when his fingers began trembling. Then he had learned how to work with leather, how to dip it and stretch it over a mold, then fill in all the hollow places with tiny scraps glued together. He would spend hours on a single pair of shoes and keep making custom adjustments until the patient's foot showed no more stress points.

Uncle Robbie lived alone in a guest room at the leprosarium—his wife had died some years before. He worked with us three or four years, training a whole platoon of Indian shoemakers. Watching him labor so tenderly over the damaged feet of leprosy patients, I could hardly imagine him in the prestigious, high-pressure environment of orthopedic surgery back in New Zealand.

He was an utterly unassuming man, and nearly everyone he met came to love him. No one ever felt sorry for Uncle Robbie—he was perhaps the most self-contented person I have ever known. He did his work for the glory of God alone.[1]

Kind of goes against what most of us believe would constitute a happy life, doesn't it? I imagine Uncle Robbie's friends and co-workers back in New Zealand thought he was crazy to go to India and minister to lepers.

"Come on, Robert," I can hear them say. "You've got it all! Prestige, money, possessions. You're out of your mind to give that all up! Why not just settle down in a nice condo by the beach and enjoy your retirement? You deserve it."

I'm sure scores of lepers in India (not to mention one writer in the suburbs of Atlanta, Georgia) are glad Uncle Robbie marched to a different drummer.

Dr. Brand's closing thoughts about this man and others like him are worth adding:

A cobbler shop and a foot clinic may seem like unpromising settings in which to learn about pleasure. Nevertheless, these are some of the people I look back upon as happy in the deepest sense. They achieved a "shalom" of the spirit powerful enough to transform pain—their own pain as well as others'. "Happy are they who bear their share of the world's pain: In the long run they will know more happiness than those who avoid it," said Jesus in J. B. Phillip's paraphrase.[2]

God came to earth not on a fiery chariot with live CNN coverage but quietly in a stable in a little village. God came to earth not with a ticker tape parade down Broadway with millions of cheering, adoring fans, but with a small gathering of shepherds, a few animals, and mom and dad. God came to earth not on a throne but in a manger.

We should have known, for God's ways are different from ours.

Jesus' closest buddy, John, recorded an incident in his book which none of the other Gospel writers mentioned.

Now before the Feast of the Passover, Jesus knowing that His hour had come that He should depart out of this world to the Father, having loved His own who were in the world, He loved them to the end. And during supper, the devil having already put into the heart of Judas Iscariot, the son of Simon, to betray Him, Jesus, knowing that the Father had given all things into His hands, and that He had come forth from God, and was going back to God, rose from supper and laid aside His garments; and taking a towel, girded Himself about. Then He poured water into the basin, and began to wash the disciples feet, and to wipe them with the towel with which He was girded (John 13:1-5).

Peter couldn't believe his eyes! When his turn came to have his feet washed by Jesus, he couldn't handle it. Washing feet was a slave's job, much too degrading for their Teacher and Lord. Peter would have none of this outrageous behavior, and he told Jesus so.

> Peter said to Him, "Never shall You wash my feet!" Jesus answered him, "If I do not wash you, you have no part with Me." Simon Peter said to Him, "Lord, not my feet only, but also my hands and my head" (John 13:8,9).

Maybe you have struggled with what living the Christian life is all about. In John 13, Jesus gave us a picture to help us understand this very thing. You can sum it up this way: *Let Jesus wash your feet* (a picture of allowing Jesus to serve us and forgive us) *and go in turn and wash the feet of others.* Here's how John put it:

> And so when He had washed their feet, and taken His garments, and reclined at the table again, He said to them, "Do you know what I have done to you? You call Me Teacher and Lord, and you are right, for so I am. If I then, the Lord and the Teacher, washed your feet, you also ought to wash one another's feet. For I gave you an example that you also should do as I did to you. Truly, truly, I say to you, a slave is not greater than his master, neither one who is sent greater than the one who sent him. If you know these things, you are blessed if you do them" (John 13:12-17).

Go and do likewise. Follow in the footsteps of the God who serves. The joy of the Lord will be your reward ... and your strength.

THE LIE TO REJECT

I reject the lie that true happiness comes from being served by others and getting others to do my will. I refuse to adopt the world's philosophy that success means having other people work for me.

THE TRUTH TO ACCEPT

I accept the truth that true happiness comes from following Jesus' example of serving others. I choose to believe this truth no matter what anyone around me says.

PRAYER FOR TODAY

Dear heavenly Father, I thank You for the example of Jesus, who did not come to be served, but to serve and to give His life a ransom for many (Matthew 20:28). Father, living a life of serving others goes against what the world says brings happiness. And, to be honest, it goes against a lot of how I feel, too. Please, open the eyes of my heart to truly know and believe that true joy comes from serving other people. I ask You to make me a servant like Jesus. And it's in His name I pray. Amen.

READ ALL ABOUT IT

Luke 9

GOING DEEPER WITH GOD

Matthew 25

A Party Hearty in Heaven

In the same way, I tell you, there is joy in the presence of the angels of God over one sinner who repents (Luke 15:10).

I couldn't believe my eyes and ears. Youth speaker Bert Robinson was talking about "love, sex, and dating" from a Christian point of view. He had just asked a group of high school guys a question and the response he got blew him and me away.

The question was, "How many of you guys think God is a prude?"

Now this was not a group of hard-cores off the streets of New York City. These were basically Christian kids from white, middle-class suburbia.

About one-fourth of the group raised their hands and said, "I do."

And these weren't timid, raise-the-hand-about-two-inches kind of raised hands. Those hands shot up and those mouths shot off. Those guys were obviously very convinced that God was in the heavenly business of zapping all possible fun out of life, especially when it comes to sex.

They definitely needed a good dose of the Bible's *Song of Solomon* to straighten out their thinking.

But it makes me wonder: How many teenagers, even Christian teenagers, have this picture of God that we used to call the "Three S's"?

Straightlaced
Sad
Somber

Now don't get me wrong. I don't think God is silly, nor do I think He winks at our sin. But neither do I think He sits up in heaven gloomy-faced with his jowls drooping down through the clouds.

One of Job's "friends", Bildad the Shuhite was trying to encourage Job in the midst of his pain. He said of God:

> He [God] will yet fill your mouth with laughter, and your lips with shouting (Job 8:21).

If God can fill a person's mouth with laughter, do you know what that means? God is into laughter. He enjoys a good (clean!) joke and a good laugh!

Heaven, contrary to most people's ideas, is a place of great joy and pleasure. Not the kind of erotic pleasure that the Muslims teach, but joy and pleasure of the purest and deepest kind. Don't believe me? Look at what King David had to say about God and heaven:

> You have made known to me the path of life; you will fill me with joy in your presence, with eternal pleasures at your right hand (Psalm 16:11 NIV).

Jesus, while He was on earth, was described this way by His Father:

> You have loved righteousness and hated wickedness; therefore God, your God, has set you above your companions by anointing you with the oil of joy (Hebrews 1:9 NIV).

What was that word used to describe Jesus? Did you catch it? Joy!

Why was Jesus the most joyful man who ever lived? Because He was the most holy! That's what Hebrews 1:9 says. Read it again. Jesus loved what was right and hated what was wrong, and *therefore* God has set Him above His companions by anointing Him with the oil of joy!

Ever since the Garden of Eden the devil has been circulating this awful rumor that God is some sort of cosmic killjoy. He basically told Eve to go ahead and eat from the forbidden fruit because God was just being mean and selfish by not letting her.

And, based upon the response of those guys at the "love, sex, and dating" seminar, Satan is still using that same slander tactic today. He whispers to us:

> God's trying to take all the fun out of life. You can't trust God; He's going to make your life miserable. The Christian life is so boooring; God doesn't let you do anything fun!

Do you ever hear people talk that way? Do you ever feel that way? Maybe you need to tune in to a party on earth and in heaven to see what life is really like in the presence of God. Let's go back to the book of Luke and see:

> Now all the tax-gatherers and the sinners were coming near Him to listen to Him. And both the Pharisees and the scribes began to grumble, saying, "This man receives sinners and eats with them." And He told them this parable, saying, "What man among you, if he has a hundred sheep and has lost one of them, does not leave the ninety-nine in the open pasture, and go after the one which is lost, until he finds it? And when he has found it, he lays it on his shoulders, rejoicing. And when he comes home, he calls together his friends and his neighbors, saying to them, 'Rejoice with me, for I have found

my sheep which was lost!' I tell you that in the same
way, there will be more joy in heaven over one sinner
who repents, than over ninety-nine righteous persons who need no repentance " (Luke 15:1-7).

Where was Jesus, by the way, when he talked to the
straightlaced, sad-and-somber Pharisees and scribes? With
a group of tax-gatherers and sinners. Do you think they were
all sitting around looking like they'd all just eaten a rotten
fig? Of course not.

Jesus was so well-known on the local social scene that
those same Jewish leaders accused Him of being a glutton
and a drunkard! (see Matthew 11:19). Now Jesus was neither of those things; He was sinless. But you don't get a rep-
utation like that by being anti-enjoyment!

Jesus just had a different and better definition of fun than
most people today. He was totally free to enjoy Himself,
people, food, music, etc. without ever going overboard.

Now on to the party in heaven. The angels are the biggest
celebrators in the whole universe! How do I know that?
Because they celebrate every time someone comes to Christ
(see today's Scripture). My friend, people are repenting of their
sins and being forgiven by Jesus all over the world every day!

I don't know about you, but I think the Christian life has
really been given a bum rap by the devil. You see, it is the
cold, mean religious people who are the cosmic killjoys. But
those who are alive and on-fire for Christ? They experience
the deepest joy and the greatest fun of all! Just ask Jesus!

THE LIE TO REJECT

*I reject the lie of Satan that the Christian life is dull and
boring and that God wants to take all the fun out of life.*

I refuse to believe the devil's deception and slander that God cannot be trusted and that real fun is found in the world of sin.

THE TRUTH TO ACCEPT

I accept the truth that Jesus was the most joyful man who ever lived and that His joy was of the deepest, greatest, and holiest kind. I know that following Him is the path to true joy.

PRAYER FOR TODAY

Dear Lord, I know that Your Word says that Jesus was "a man of sorrows and acquainted with grief" (Isaiah 53:3), but I thank You that He was also a Man of the greatest joy. In fact, Jesus experienced the full range of holy, human emotions in perfect freedom. I want to be like Him, Lord and be free to have fun, and feel the joy that comes from a life of loving what is right and hating what is wrong. Please set me free from the lies and fears in my life that hold me back from enjoying life like He did. I look forward to experiencing in a deeper, "riper" way the fruit of the Spirit, which includes joy, as I walk with You by faith. In Jesus' name I pray. Amen.

READ ALL ABOUT IT

Luke 15

GOING DEEPER WITH GOD

Matthew 26

YOU DON'T MESS AROUND WITH GOD

He began to teach and say to them, "Is it not written, 'My house shall be called a house of prayer for all the nations'? But you have made it a robbers' den" (Mark 11:17).

When it comes to action-packed movies, the first Indiana Jones film, *Raiders of the Lost Ark,* is a classic. In it, Harrison Ford plays the part of a professor of archaeology who also happens to have a nose for treasure hunting. His quest? To find the holy "ark of the covenant" built during the time of Moses.

There's just one problem: The Nazis are after it, too.

Professor Jones wants to find the ark for the sheer historical value of it (not to mention the fame it would bring him!). The Germans want to find it because they believe the nation that owns the ark controls the world.

After many harrowing adventures and narrow escapes, Indiana finds the ark. Unfortunately, the Nazis find him and take the ark.

My favorite scene in the movie takes place in a storage area where the ark is being kept inside a wooden box. On the outside of the crate is stamped the symbol of Nazi power, the swastika. Suddenly the power of God comes from the ark and simply burns out the swastika so that it is no longer visible on the side of the box. That is just a taste of the power of God that is to come.

The climax of the film occurs when the Nazi officer approaches the ark to open it. He's practically drooling over the power he feels is now at his fingertips. Is he ever in for a surprise!

Opening the ark turns out to be a really dumb move because a host of destroying angels stream out once the lid is lifted. The angels wipe out the Germans, and only Indiana and his gorgeous companion are spared because they refused to look at the opened ark.

You might be amazed to know that the movie is based on some historical facts.

The scene took place during the time of the prophet/judge Samuel. The real ark of the covenant had been captured by the Philistines but it became a real headache for them, so they sent it back to Israel.

The Philistines put it on a wooden cart pulled by two cows. As the ark came back to the town of Beth Shemesh, the Israelites were beside themselves with joy. Some Levites took the ark off the cart, chopped up the wood of the cart to build a fire, and sacrificed the cows to the Lord. So far so good.

Then they made a big mistake. First Samuel 6:19,20 NIV tells the story:

> But God struck down some of the men of Beth Shemesh, putting seventy of them to death because they had looked into the ark of the LORD. The people mourned because of the heavy blow the LORD had dealt them, and the men of Beth Shemesh asked, "Who can stand in the presence of the LORD, this holy God?"

Why was God so ticked off at the people who looked inside the ark? After all, they had probably never seen it before and it was only natural to be curious, right? Maybe they wanted to make sure the Ten Commandments, Aaron's rod, and the golden jar of manna were still inside. What's wrong with that?

The answer is simple: God is holy, and in His holy law He had already clearly declared the ark of the covenant to be off-limits to unholy eyes.

The people were guilty of treating something holy as though it were trivial. And God will not stand for that.

In Acts 5 Ananias and Sapphira sold a piece of property. Wanting to appear more spiritual than they actually were, they presented a portion of the money from the sale but told Peter that they were giving it all. God saw right through their lie and struck them both dead.

The result? Great fear came upon the whole church (Acts 5:11). The people learned a lesson: You don't mess around with God. Ananias and Sapphira learned the hard way.

In Corinthians 11 the apostle Paul warned against taking the Lord's supper in an unworthy manner—treating the holy as though it were trivial. God was not pleased with that casual, irreverent attitude, and for this reason many among the Corinthian believers were weak, sick or dead! (See 1 Corinthians 11:30.)

Even the usually gentle, kind Jesus erupted in anger when He saw the moneychangers and merchants setting up shop in the temple area. Mark wrote:

> And they came to Jerusalem. And He entered the temple and began to cast out those who were buying and selling in the temple, and overturned the tables of the moneychangers and the seats of those who were selling doves; and He would not permit

anyone to carry goods through the temple. And He began to teach and say to them, "Is it not written, 'My house shall be called a house of prayer for all the nations'? But you have made it a robbers' den" (Mark 11:15-17).

The holy temple of God, a place designed for worship and prayer, had been turned into a marketplace. The holy had been treated as though it were trivial.

As you begin (or end) this day in the presence of the Holy One, and especially when you prepare to take the Lord's Supper, this question should be foremost on your mind:

Lord, am I in any way treating the holy things of God as though they were common and trivial?

Here is just a sampling of how we might do that:

By considering going to church just one of many possible options for Sunday, along with sleeping in, going to the mall, or going to see a movie.

By being rude or distracting during youth group meetings or church worship services.

By making fun of or gossiping about your pastor, youth pastor or other church leaders.

By treating the Bible as just another book, filled with errors, or by ignoring what God says in His Word for you to do.

By using your body, the temple of the Holy Spirit, for sexual sin.

Charles Colson hit the nail right on the head when he wrote:

We need to know the fear of the Lord—the overwhelming, compelling awe and reverence of a holy God. The fear of the Lord is the beginning of wisdom: It provides the right perspective on God's sovereign rule over all creation; the sense of God's power and perfection that dwarfs mere men and women, that causes them to bow and worship and glory in His amazing grace. [1]

Amen. God has by His wonderful grace turned ordinary human beings like you and me into saints, holy ones, children of the living God. How dare we then treat what God has declared holy as if it were trivial?

THE LIE TO REJECT

I reject the lie that my attitude toward the things of God doesn't matter just so long as I go to church and do other Christian things. I refuse to treat holy things and holy people as if they were trivial or unimportant or to be taken for granted.

THE TRUTH TO ACCEPT

I accept the truth that God is holy and not to be taken lightly. I realize that He does get angry when I make fun of or take for granted His Word, His church, His spiritual leaders, and most of all Himself.

PRAYER FOR TODAY

Dear heavenly Father, I know that there have been too many times when I have treated the things of God too casually, as though they were not important. Please forgive me for taking for granted Your Word, Your church, my pastor and youth leader, and especially You. "Teach

*me your way, O LORD, and I will walk in your truth;
give me an undivided heart, that I may fear your name. I
will praise you, O Lord my God, with all my heart; I will
glorify your name forever. For great is your love toward
me; you have delivered me from the depths of the grave"
(Psalm 86:11-13 NIV). In Jesus' name. Amen.*

Read All About It

1 Samuel 5,6

Going Deeper with God

Matthew 27

THANK GOD!

Love your enemies, and do good, and lend, expecting nothing in return; and your reward will be great, and you will be sons of the Most High; for He Himself is kind to ungrateful and evil men (Luke 6:35).

When I was growing up I hated anything to do with church, God, or religion. I would intentionally oversleep on Sunday mornings and dink around trying to find my dress shoes until my exasperated mother left for church without me. Sometimes I would pretend I was sick. Then when everyone was gone I would flip on the tube and watch cartoons.

At meals our family rarely gave thanks, except at holidays like Thanksgiving, Christmas, and Easter. Then I would impatiently bow my head with the rest of my family and relatives and quickly mumble the prayer:

> *God is great, God is good,*
> *And we thank Him for our food.*
> *By His hand we all are fed;*
> *Give us, Lord, our daily bread.*
> *In Jesus' name. Amen.*

And then I would greedily gulp down the grub in front of me, practically growling at anyone who would dare ask me to pass something to him.

As I look at that prayer, a couple things hit me. First, it is a very good prayer. There's nothing wrong with it at all.

It honors God and admits our dependence upon Him. It even rhymes, making it easier to remember.

Second, I don't think God listened to a word I prayed, because I had no relationship with Jesus. I said the words *In Jesus' name, Amen*, but I didn't mean them. And I "gave thanks," or at least that's what the prayer said, but my heart was not thankful at all.

As far as I knew, the turkey came from a local turkey farm. The mashed potatoes and gravy came from the grocery store and my mom cooked them. The pumpkin pie came from Aunt...and so on. From my point of view God had absolutely nothing to do with it at all.

And that brings me to my last observation about the prayer. Even though my heart was not right with God at all, He still provided. Every holiday we would have a huge spread of food. We never lacked for anything. Why is that? I see it now. It is because "He Himself is kind to evil and ungrateful men." Now I see why we called it *saying grace.*

Grace is one of those spiritual words that is easy to throw around without really understanding what it means. In a nutshell, it means this: *God does good things to people who don't deserve it.* Psalm 145:8,9 puts it this way:

> The LORD is gracious and merciful, slow to anger and great in lovingkindness. The LORD is good to all, and His mercies are over all His works.

Did you catch that? By nature, God is full of grace and mercy and is good to everybody and everything. Now obviously God does not treat all people equally, for some have much while others have little. But God *is* good to all, and in many more ways than we usually notice. Jesus put it this way in His famous Sermon on the Mount:

I say to you, love your enemies and pray for those who persecute you, in order that you may be sons of your Father who is in heaven; for He causes His sun to rise on the evil and the good, and sends rain on the righteous and the unrighteous (Matthew 5:44,45).

Every beat of our heart and every breath we breathe should be a reminder to us that God is good. Even now I'm reminded to give thanks for my fingers that are typing these words, for my eyes that can clearly see what's on my computer screen, for my back that is *not* sore today, allowing me to sit up and write, etc. But how often do we take those basic things of life for granted—until we are in pain or in danger of losing them!

Think about it for a moment. Just look around the room where you're reading today's devotional. The ceiling. The walls. The floor. The furniture. Windows. Curtains. Light. Heat. And that's probably just the beginning of what is around you.

Why not pause for a moment and whisper a quiet *Thank You, Lord* as your eyes move slowly from one thing around you to the next.

To be honest with you, I felt kind of "blah" today. It's the day after a holiday and I'm not excited about getting back to work. My stomach feels yucky, my neck is sore, and I've been kind of irritated with my family. I don't feel particularly spiritual.

What I needed was to practice what I preach. And so that's exactly what I did. I started looking around my office, giving thanks for the things I saw, being reminded of how the Lord had provided them. It's amazing how just a few minutes of genuine thanksgiving can get your eyes off yourself and lift your spirits. Maybe that's why the Lord prompted Paul to write:

> Rejoice always; pray without ceasing; in everything give thanks; for this is God's will for you in Christ Jesus (1 Thessalonians 5:16-18).

Feeling a little "down in the dumps" spiritually today? Maybe, like me, you had developed a slight case of ingrown eyeballs—getting your eyes on yourself and your problems and off of God. Maybe, like me, you need to just be reminded that *God is great, God is good* and to burst out of your straitjacket of self-pity and thank God for what you *do* have! I like God's advice given through Psalm 100. I need it today; how about you?

> Shout joyfully to the LORD, all the earth. Serve the LORD with gladness; come before Him with joyful singing. Know that the LORD Himself is God; it is He who has made us, and not we ourselves; we are His people and the sheep of His pasture. Enter His gates with thanksgiving, and His courts with praise. Give thanks to Him; bless His name. For the LORD is good; His lovingkindness is everlasting, and His faithfulness to all generations (Psalm 100:1-5).

Thє Lιє το Rєjєcτ

I reject the lie that God has been unkind to me. I refuse to focus on the things I do not have and develop a depressed, resentful, or self- pitying spirit.

THE TRUTH TO ACCEPT

I accept the truth that God is good and kind to me, even when I do not notice or appreciate it. I choose to give thanks for the many blessings He has given me today, none of which I deserve.

PRAYER FOR TODAY

Dear heavenly Father, thank You for all the things You have given me. As I think about that I am amazed at Your greatness and goodness! Please forgive me for my ungrateful, demanding spirit. As painful as it is to admit, I confess that I am pretty spoiled. I don't handle pain or discomfort very well and I struggle with being content with what I have. I choose today to walk in the power of the Holy Spirit and ask You, Lord, to develop a rejoicing, praying, thankful spirit in me. Thank You for Your continual goodness to me even when I do not notice or even care what You do for me. Most of all, I thank You for giving Jesus to live on earth, to die for my sins and to rise from the dead so that I could be forgiven and have new life. Help me never to take that for granted. In Jesus' name. I gratefully pray, Amen.

READ ALL ABOUT IT

Psalm 136

GOING DEEPER WITH GOD

Matthew 28

COUNT ON IT

You both precede and follow me, and place your hand of blessing on my head (Psalm 139:5 TLB).

I should have known my ministry trip to Spain was going to be "out of the ordinary" based on the way it all began—on the lawn of a beautiful hotel in the foothills of Southern California's San Bernardino mountains.

While serving on the staff of Campus Crusade for Christ's high school ministry, I took a day with the Lord at that ministry's headquarters, Arrowhead Springs. I had spent the day enjoying the flowers and the lush, green grass of the grounds, reading about foreign missions and dreaming of being a missionary myself someday. It was a much-needed day away from my ministry to Riverside, California, high school students.

Suddenly a prayer began to form in my mind: *Lord, where could I go this summer on the foreign mission field?* Almost as soon as I had prayed the prayer, another idea came to me: *Walk down to the international office and see what they've got available.*

Filled with anticipation, I walked through the sun-drenched gardens of flowers to that office. I introduced myself and the somewhat-surprised secretary pulled out a piece of paper.

"Just today we received a request for someone experienced in speaking to high school students to do a conference for youth in Spain. Are you interested?"

After explaining how God had been working in my heart that day, we both agreed that the Lord was in it. She contacted the staff in Spain with the good news and I began to make preparations to go. I was even able to take a high school student with me!

Just because God calls you to do something, however, doesn't mean that everything will be easy. What it does mean, though, is that you can hang in there and walk by faith, knowing that He *will* provide. As it turned out, I was to learn that lesson really fast.

When my friend and I arrived at the international airport in Madrid, it was very late. In fact, the airport was preparing to close. We were confident, though, that we would be greeted by a grateful group of Spanish Christians eager to take us to our nice, comfortable room. So, without a care, we strolled through the "Customs" and "Immigration" areas, picked up our suitcases, and prepared to meet our ride.

But there was no one there. No banners proclaiming "Welcome Americanos!" Not even a single Spaniard with a cheap little sign saying, "MILLER." Nothing. Not even a message over the PA system.

Man, was I hacked off. Here we raised all this money to come over and speak at their conference and they didn't even have the decency to pick us up. Boy, was this missionary stuff for the birds, I thought.

Beyond that, we were about to be shooed out of the airport at four o'clock in the morning.

On the verge of despair, I remembered the phone number. A couple at my church had given me the name and phone number of some American missionary friends of theirs who lived in Madrid. Politely I had stuffed the information in my pocket, silently thinking, "I'm not going to call these people. I don't even know them."

A few minutes later (after finding some Spanish coins and figuring out how to use the phones) I had the missionaries on the line, begging them to pick us up and rescue us from the closing airport. What a strong, brave missionary I was...not!

Graciously, this family picked us up, took us into their home, let us stay with them a few days (while we overcame jet lag), gave us a tour of Madrid, and drove us to the bus station so we could get on to our destination. My airport panic was totally uncalled for. God indeed had called me to Spain and He was going to take care of me.

A few weeks later I learned another aspect of God's faithful care. Toward the end of my mission trip to Spain, the leaders of the conference took me to a small town to buy gifts for my family back home. I had carefully budgeted my spending money and so I knew how much I had available to spend. The deals on pottery were unbelievable, as was the beauty of the craftsmanship. I had a great time picking out things for my parents and other relatives, and I was excited about seeing their faces when they opened their gifts.

A day or so before we were to ride the bus back to Madrid to catch our flight, I was walking near the conference site by myself. There lying on the ground was the Spanish equivalent of 40 dollars. I couldn't believe it! I looked around. There was no one there but me. I could keep the money!

A few days later my friend and I said our goodbyes, and we were dropped off at the bus station. When I walked up to the ticket counter I got the shock of my life. What I had figured to pay for the return bus ticket was way off. It was much more expensive than I had figured. You guessed it . . . by about 40 dollars!

From beginning to end, that trip was one big teaching lesson from God.

What a joy (and relief!) it was to plop down in the seat on the bus, knowing we were on our way to the airport and then home. It had been an adventure, to be sure, and in many ways (more than I have room to write about here) very difficult. But had it all been smooth sailing I would never have experienced the faithful hand of God meeting my needs long before I even knew I had them. I began to see that when God calls, He provides. You can count on it!

The writer of Psalm 139 knew that truth well when he wrote:

> O Lord, you have examined my heart and know everything about me. You know when I sit or stand. When far away you know my every thought. You chart the path ahead of me, and tell me where to stop and rest. Every moment you know where I am. You know what I am going to say before I even say it. You both precede and follow me, and place your hand of blessing on my head. This is too glorious, too wonderful to believe!

> I can never be lost to your Spirit! I can never get away from my God! If I go up to heaven, you are there; if I go down to the place of the dead, you are there. If I ride the morning winds to the farthest oceans, even there your hand will guide me, your strength will support me (Psalm 139:1-10 TLB).

Where has God called you to be today? At school as usual? At home doing chores or babysitting a younger brother or sister? At a game competing or an auditorium performing? At a job working? On a plane headed for a far-away state or foreign country?

Wherever you are and wherever you go, be assured that God is with you now and has already gone before you to prepare the way for you. So why not turn the ordinary and humdrum into an adventure today? After all, *every* day can be an adventure when you live with the reality that God is in it!

The "Make Today An Adventure of Faith" Project

Fill out the chart below, listing the activities you have planned for the day ahead on the left. On the right, write out a prayer, asking God to do something supernatural in and through each activity. Then write down later how God answered your prayers.

Today's Activities	Prayer of Faith
1.	
2.	
3.	
4.	
5.	
6.	

Prayer for Today

Dear heavenly Father, I thank You that I don't have to be flying to a foreign country on a missions project to live by faith. I can do that today right here. Open my eyes to the ways in which You can show Your power and presence this day at my school, in my home and in all the other places I hang out. Please give me strength to step out in faith and tell others about my faith in You. Help me to see the needs of people around me so that I can pray for them and say and do kind things to encourage them. I want my life to be an adventure of faith, not a day-in and day-out drudgery of the same old thing. Help me to believe that "everywhere God is, there is an adventure waiting to happen." I pray in faith in Jesus' name. Amen.

READ ALL ABOUT IT
Psalm 139

GOING DEEPER WITH GOD
1 Peter 1

ACCEPT OR EXCEPT?

Accept one another, just as Christ also accepted us to the glory of God (Romans 15:7).

My wife, Shirley, is from the South. Now if you happen to be from the South too, don't get mad at me for this story. I'm not an arrogant Yankee who happens to believe all Southerners are country bumpkins in bare feet, but it did take me some time to get used to the way y'all talk!

Early in our marriage I noticed that Shirley really liked the word "good." Now there's nothing wrong with the word "good." It's a good word. She just happened to use it a lot. At least it seemed that way to me. And when she said "good" it turned into a three-syllable word, "goo-oo-ood."

You know—"Mmm, that pie was really gooood!" Or, "Didn't you like that TV show? I thought it was so gooood." And, "Let's go outside, the weather is really gooood today."

It got to the point where I started to shudder whenever she would say the "g" word. It was really getting on my nerves, so I decided to come to my wife's rescue. I became a walking thesaurus, with suggestions like: *Honey, have you ever thought to say, "Mmm, that pie was really delicious?" Or, "Didn't you like that TV show? I thought it was so entertaining." And, "Let's go outside, the weather is really pleasant today."*

It didn't work. I still got the "good's" constantly and I was as irritated as ever.

Then one day the Lord gently spoke to my heart: "Rich, do you accept your wife just as she is or only when she uses a *good*, wide vocabulary?"

The Lord got me good that day and I had to repent of my sin. I wasn't accepting Shirley unconditionally; I was accepting her on the condition that she didn't use the word "good."

How silly, you might be thinking, making such a big deal out of a little word. You're right, it was silly, but it was driving a serious wedge between us.

Now, years later, you might wonder, "Does your wife still use the word 'good' as much as she used to?"

You know, I honestly don't know if she does or not. But what's far more important is that I don't care.

Shirley is the most wonderful wife and mother I could ever ask for. She's kind, considerate, hardworking, affectionate, fun, romantic, great with the kids, you name it. I love her except...

She has this habit of leaving lights on in rooms when she leaves and she sometimes makes messes when she cooks and... One day after enduring five years of this stuff I decided to be helpful once again. I came up with a sheet entitled "Ten Helpful Hints For a Happy Home." It included such wisdom as "If you are done with it... *put it away.*" "If you leave the room... *turn it off.*" And so on. You get the idea.

The two most helpful hints for a happy home were really:

1. Rich, don't give that stupid sheet to Shirley!

and

2. Keep your big mouth shut and be glad for the things she does well!

Unfortunately, I didn't follow those last two bits of advice and I proudly presented my version of the Ten Commandments to Shirley. Then I stood back to watch her reaction. I expected her to put them on the refrigerator and praise me for my great wisdom.

Instead, she cried.

And I put the "Ten Helpful Hints for a Happy Home" in my pile of illustrations. File it under "Stories of what *not* to do in marriage!"

What was wrong with my wonderful advice? Weren't those ten helpful principles for keeping a house clean? Sure they were, for a first-grader. Well, wasn't I just trying to help my wife improve in an area of weakness in her life? Yeah, but with three kids all under the age of four clutching at her legs all day I should've applauded her for even having the energy to get out of bed!

You see, the Bible says we are to "carry each other's burdens, and in this way . . . fulfill the law of Christ" (Galatians 6:2 NIV). What law was the apostle Paul writing about? The law of love.

When I gave that sheet to Shirley, she didn't feel loved, and she certainly didn't feel accepted. She didn't have a sense at all that I was carrying her incredible workload along with her. She felt like I had just dumped a new load on her already-breaking back!

All too often we communicate to the people close to us a love that sounds like "I love you if you do _____ or don't do _____."

What an incredible thing to realize that God doesn't treat us that way at all! God says, "I love you." No strings attached. No fine print hidden at the bottom of the contract. No ifs, ands, or buts. He just loves us as we are, period.

Believe me, if God wanted to come up with a list of conditions for His love and acceptance of us, He could come up with a doozy. Every little part of our lives is "open and laid bare" before Him (Hebrews 4:13). He could make a list of all our faults, errors, character flaws, personality quirks, weaknesses, you name it!

But the beauty of God's love and acceptance is that He doesn't want to. He's too busy being in love with His children to hold our failures against us.

Does that mean God tolerates sin in our lives? No, He doesn't tolerate sin. But He forgives it and loves us in spite of it. And He puts us on His program to change the wrong things in our lives, while loving us completely and accepting us perfectly all through that process.

If you are in Christ and Christ is in you:

> Jesus loves you right now as much as the Father loves Jesus! (Check out John 15:9 if you think it's too good to be true.)

> There isn't anything you can do to cause God to love you more! (Even reading the Bible, praying, witnessing, going to church, and giving money do not "win" more of God's love)

> There isn't anything you can do to cause God to love you less! (He loves you the same before, during, and after you sin. He loves you the same when you are sinning as when you are not.)

Now some people might get really angry at what I just wrote. They might be thinking, "If you tell people that kind of stuff, they'll just go out and sin more!"

Well, some people might, I suppose. People who are always looking for an excuse to sin might respond that way. But I don't think most people would react like that. Why not? Because people are longing to be loved and accepted in the way the Father loves His children.

How about you? Have you lived your Christian life with this uncomfortable sense that you were just "not doing enough for God"? That God expects you to jump through all these spiritual hoops in order to gain His approval? Have you felt like God was constantly disappointed in you? Or that He loves and accepts you *except* when you commit that sin you've been struggling with for what seems like forever?

Take heart. God's love is not spelled *except*. It's spelled *accept*. Period.

The Lie to Reject

I reject the lie that God's love and acceptance of me are based on my spiritual performance. I refuse to accept the devil's discouraging picture of God as being a frowning, disapproving perfectionist.

The Truth to Accept

I accept the truth that God loves me and accepts me perfectly in Christ. I choose to accept that kind of pure love into my life even though I have never been loved like that before.

Prayer for Today

Most loving, accepting heavenly Father, I know that it is the shed blood of Jesus cleansing me from my sin that makes me acceptable before Your holy presence. And I also realize that there is much that I do that is not holy and much of my character that is not yet very Christlike. But today I want to just bathe in the light of Your perfect love and acceptance. I want it to warm up my soul and thaw out the cold, hard places in my heart so that I can love other people with Your kind of love. It seems too good to be true that You love me just the way I am, but Your Word says it's true. May this incredible truth set me free to love You deeply. In Jesus' name. Amen.

READ ALL ABOUT IT
2 Samuel 9

GOING DEEPER WITH GOD
1 Peter 2

UNQUENCHABLE LOVE

You shall not worship any other god, for the LORD,
whose name is Jealous, is a jealous God (Exodus 34:14).

A what? A *jealous* God? How can that be? Isn't jealousy
a sin? I mean, it's listed in Galatians 5:19-21 along with stuff
like immorality, idolatry, sorcery, and drunkenness. Besides,
doesn't 1 Corinthians 13:4 say that love is not jealous? And
doesn't the Bible say that "God is love"?

And what in the world is this verse talking about when
it says God's "name is Jealous"? I mean, I can understand
saying "His name is Holy" or "His name is Powerful" or
"Love" or "Justice," but *Jealous?* Isn't jealousy that petty
quality of being suspicious of a rival, as in "I saw that guy
smiling at you, and if he tries it again, I'll tear his face off!"

Jealousy brings back memories of cruel, demanding,
overly-controlling soap opera men insecure over losing their
girlfriends. Or of cheap, sleazy paperback books with
scheming, catty women trying to get their men to notice
them more by flirting around with other guys.

Jealousy is gross stuff. Whenever you're around it (or in
it!) you feel like some kind of gooey, smelly slime is sticking
to you and won't peel off. Surely God would not have a part
in that kind of thing, would He?

Surely you're right. He wouldn't, and doesn't.

But the fact remains that the Bible reveals that God *is*
indeed a jealous God, to the point that His very name is

Jealous. Let me ask a few questions to try to shed some light on this rarely-talked-about part of God's character.

What would you think of a husband who knew that his wife was messing around with other guys but never did anything about it? He never confronted his wife with the problem, but just sat around watching TV while she had her affairs. Would you respect a man like that? Would you say that he loved his wife very much?

How about this one:

How would you feel if you were playing on a team and one of the other players was always goofing off in practice and during the games? The player's behavior was distracting to everybody else, keeping the team from really doing their best. Your coach saw what was going on but didn't take action to correct the situation.

In fact, it got so bad that this player would spend half the time over with the other team, being buddy-buddy with them! Still the coach did nothing. Would you want to play for a coach like that? Wouldn't you completely lose respect for him or her?

Are you beginning to see how jealousy at times is a good, positive, and even necessary quality to possess?

A husband who did not become jealous when his wife was running around with other guys would not be much of a husband at all. You could rightly conclude that he had little genuine love and concern for his wife.

A coach who did not become jealous and protective of his team when one player became a distraction and danger to their overall well-being would be unqualified for the job.

When it comes to His people (all believers in Christ) God has a deep, passionate, caring, protective love—like a good husband has for his wife. Catch a glimpse of the kind of commitment He has to you and me in this passage of Scripture from Song of Solomon:

> Put me like a seal over your heart, like a seal on your arm. For love is as strong as death, jealousy is as severe as Sheol; its flashes are flashes of fire, the very

> flame of the LORD. Many waters cannot quench love,
> nor will rivers overflow it; if a man were to give all
> the riches of his house for love, it would be utterly
> despised (Song of Solomon 8:6,7).

An unquenchable love! How does it make you feel to
see that God's love for you is as intense and passionate as
that? It should make you feel really special, because you are!
In fact, Isaiah 54:5 says, "For your husband is your Maker,
whose name is the LORD of hosts; and your Redeemer is the
Holy One of Israel, who is called the God of all the earth."

God is our husband and we are His bride. He loves us
deeply and He knows that no one or no thing can ever love
us and protect us like He can. So it should not surprise us
that He will tolerate no rivals. Our natural response should
be to love *Him* with all our heart, soul, strength, and mind
(Luke 10:27). And that is exactly what God expects. The
beginning of the Ten Commandments sets the stage for how
serious God is about our loyalty to Him:

> I am the LORD your God, who brought you out of
> the land of Egypt, out of the house of slavery. You
> shall have no other gods before Me. You shall not
> make for yourself an idol. . . . You shall not worship
> them or serve them; for I, the LORD your God, am a
> jealous God (Exodus 20:2-5).

Usually at this point we breathe a sigh of relief, wipe
the sweat off our foreheads, and say, "Whew, that was close!
I thought for a minute that verse was going to be for me,
but I don't worship idols."

But idols are much more than little statues of Buddha or
other gods that people worship in temples or at altars. An idol
can be just about anything that comes between you and God.

A sport can be an idol, and so can a music group. The
pursuit of excellent grades can be an idol, and so can pop-

ularity. Certainly a relationship with a boyfriend or girl-friend can be an idol as well.

How can you tell if something or someone has become an idol?

Ask God to show you! He will.

But here's one key thought from Exodus 20:5: *God warns us not to worship or serve anything except Him.* To serve something means to allow it to control us and continually occupy our thoughts and direct our actions.

Maybe it would be a good idea to let God give you a long, hard look at yourself so you can see what is really important to you. Where does God *really* show up on that list? I'm not talking about where He *should* be, but if you're really honest, where He *is.* I hope He really is "number one," beyond a shadow of a doubt. But if He's not, now is the time to do something about it.

Don't wait for God to take direct action against the other gods in your life. One day He will if you don't, because He is a jealous God. But it will be much easier on you if you do it *now.* I know from experience.

Get rid of anything that is evil. And even if anything *good* has become more important to you than your relationship with Jesus, put it where it belongs. Don't let it become your master; make it your servant. Put God back up at the top of the list where He belongs . . . on His throne!

THE "SMASHING THE IDOLS" PROJECT

The last verse in the book of First John warns, "Little children, guard yourselves from idols" (1 John 5:21). Realize that you have an enemy who wants to lure you away from loving, trusting, and worshiping Jesus with all your heart. Paul wrote these critical words in 2 Corinthians 11:2,3:

> I am jealous for you with a godly jealousy; for I betrothed you to one husband, that to Christ I might present you as a pure virgin. But I am afraid, lest as the serpent deceived Eve by his craftiness, your minds should be led astray from the simplicity and purity of devotion to Christ.

If the devil can get you to be devoted to anything or anyone above Jesus Christ, he will. As you begin this short project, pray the following prayer:

> Dear Lord, please show me anything or anyone, including myself, that has become more important to me than You. I want to regain that simple and pure devotion to Jesus. If there is anything at all blocking that, please bring that to my mind now. In Jesus' name. Amen.

For each of the things or people that the Lord brings to your mind, pray the following prayer from your heart. It is important that you pray the following prayer *out loud:*

> *Dear heavenly Father, I know that* (name the thing or person) *has become more important to me than You. I'm sorry that this has become an idol and a god to me, so I remove it from the center of my life. You are indeed a jealously loving God, so I once again put You on the throne of my life, where You belong. In Jesus' name. Amen.*

Read All About It

Hosea 14

Going Deeper with God

1 Peter 3

A LOAD OFF MY MIND

This is the love of God, that we keep His commandments; and His commandments are not burdensome (1 John 5:3).

I've had six dogs in my life, but I'd have to say my favorite is the one I have now. He is a purebred Siberian husky, nearly 12 years old, fat and lazy, but as lovable as a teddy bear. Since I live in the South, where the "dog days of summer" aren't fit for a dog, I keep him at my parents' house in Pennsylvania. There he spends July and August sleeping by the air conditioning vents in their den. A dog's life ain't so bad after all!

Originally we had wanted to name him Graywolf of the Brandywine. We thought that sounded pretty impressive, but his name came back from the AKC officially as Graywolf VIII. That's too much of a mouthful to say, so we started calling him "Graywolf" for short . . . then just "Wolf." Now he's known by my kids as "Wolfie."

I had dreams that he would become Graywolf of the Brandywine, Conqueror of the North, Master of the Ice and Snow. Never happened. Instead, he's just Wolfie, Shedder of Massive Amounts of Fur, Licker of the Bowl of Ice Cream. Oh well, we love him anyway.

When Wolf was a pup we discovered something unpleasant about huskies. They're kind of like Labrador retrievers in that they think everybody's yard is *their* yard.

In other words, they love to roam. So early on we realized that we would have to put a fence around the yard to keep him in.

Unfortunately, huskies also love to dig and can jump really high, so a normal fence just wasn't going to cut it in his case.

So we chose what's called an "invisible fence." It's expensive, but effective . . . usually. Here's how our invisible fence works.

A wire was placed underground around the border of the yard and connected to a radio transmitter in the basement of my parent's house. A small, battery-operated radio receiver attached to a leather collar was put around Wolf's neck. The idea was that when Wolf wandered near the edge of the property, a little beeping sound would warn him to back off. If he didn't, a mild electric shock would jolt him. *Then* he would definitely move back!

Now before you think we're some kind of heartless, ex-Nazi war criminals getting our jollies out of torturing poor puppies, let me explain. I touched the electrodes and allowed myself to get jolted, just to make sure it wasn't dangerous. Believe me, it's unpleasant, but not harmful to dog or man!

When Wolf first became introduced to the system, it took a little time for him to get used to it. He would wander around the yard, sniffing things and generally acting like a puppy. When he got too close to the underground wire, his "beeper" would go off. But Wolf would think there was a mouse or mole on the ground and try to pounce on it. Two seconds later he'd get zapped. Then he'd yipe and run back toward the house.

It was painful for me to watch him get jolted, but I knew it was for his own good. You see, Wolf was clueless of the danger out in the street: cars. And even though it was a little painful for him to get shocked, it was nothing compared to getting hit by a car.

I'm sure there were times when he was hurt and even confused by this strange pain that hit him every time he moved to the edge of our land. But eventually he learned how far to go, and that safety was found near the house.

The alternative to the invisible fenced-in yard would have been to put Wolf on a chain or keep him in a pen. But by learning his master's system, he had much more freedom to run and roam around the yard. He's happier and so are we.

Sometimes when we come to God's Word we see a whole bunch of "do's and don'ts." I remember as a young Christian thinking that it was absolutely impossible to even remember all God's commands, let alone keep them. The Christian life became for me a horrible prison of "Do this! Don't do that!" like walls of a jail cell closing in on me and shrinking away my freedom.

Do you ever feel that way? Then take heart. Today's Scripture is meant to sweep away that closed-in, shut-in kind of feeling. First John 5:3 says that God is not trying to dump an unbearable load on our backs. "His commandments are not burdensome," the Bible assures us. In other words, what God has called us to do is really pretty basic and simple.

The Jewish people of Jesus' day probably felt a lot like I did. There seemed to be a sacrifice or ritual or command or ceremony for every minute of the day. Some of those things God had told them to do, but a lot of it was created by men. By the time Jesus came on the scene, following the Jewish religion must have been about as pleasant as wearing a heavy plastic warm-up suit inside a sauna!

That's why Jesus' words to the people must have felt like a dive into a crystal-clear cool swimming pool on a hot August afternoon:

> Come to Me, all who are weary and heavy-laden, and I will give you rest. Take My yoke upon you, and learn from Me, for I am gentle and humble in heart; and you shall find rest for your souls. For My yoke is easy, and My load is light (Matthew 11:28-30).

The Christian life becomes a heavy load when we think we have to keep juggling a thousand spiritual balls at once, and if we drop one, look out! We can feel like such a failure, full of guilt and shame over all our faults.

But here's some good news: God never intended for us to live that way! He wants us to stop trying to live the Christian life in our own strength and in our own wisdom. He wants us to let Jesus teach us and lead us and strengthen us to obey His commands.

You see, the Christian life is not you and me trying on our own to act like Jesus. Good luck! I've tried it and it doesn't work. That would be like me trying to play basketball like Michael Jordan. It would be a complete joke.

The Christian life is you and me trusting *Jesus*, who lives inside of us, to change us from the inside out and make us more and more like Him. That's a whole different ball game. That's a ball game I can enjoy. That's a ball game I can *win!*

I don't know if you feel this way or not, but for me, that's a load off my mind!

THE LIE TO REJECT

I reject the lie that the Christian life is me trying somehow to obey God's commands and follow Jesus in my own strength and with my own wisdom. I completely reject that lie and call it what it is: legalism!

The Truth to Accept

I gratefully accept the truth that the Christian life is a life of faith in Jesus, relying upon Him and trusting in His strength, wisdom, and love to enable me to walk with God and obey His commands.

Prayer for Today

Dear Lord, I have to admit that sometimes I get so tired trying to live a good life. I fall flat on my face so often and am tempted to throw in the towel and give it up. Now I see that I was right all along! I can't live the Christian life! Only You can, Jesus, because the Christian life is Your life. Right now I choose to stop trying to walk with You in my own power, and I confess my attempts as pride and foolishness. I choose now to rely upon the great power, wisdom, and love of the Spirit of Christ who lives in me. I know that Your commandments are not a pain in the neck, but that with You leading my life I will indeed find rest for my soul. In Jesus' name. Amen.

Read All About It

John 15

Going Deeper with God

1 Peter 4

A LIFETIME GUARANTEE

It is God who makes both us and you stand firm in Christ. He anointed us, set his seal of ownership on us, and put his Spirit in our hearts as a deposit, guaranteeing what is to come (2 Corinthians 1:21,22 NIV).

I used to be really afraid of heights. I would get jittery driving across high bridges in a car. If I had to ride a chairlift at a ski resort, my insides would go bananas. Those things are not a problem for me anymore, but to overcome my fear I had to face it head-on.

One such time was a few years ago when I went rock climbing. As I stared up at this 30-foot-high cliff, I began to sweat. Others who were experienced at belaying explained to me how safe it was. Yeah, right. The guy who was climbing right before me fell about ten feet flat on his back because his belayer was a little be-lazy. That really bolstered my confidence. Fortunately, neither the climber nor the belayer (on whom the climber landed!) were hurt.

Well, like a nightmare come true, it was finally my turn to go up. All kinds of fears ricocheted around in my brain:
What if I have that same belayer?
What if I can't find a foothold or handhold?
Am I going to look like a complete dork up there?
Am I strong enough to do this?
What if I panic?
What if I fall?

Will anyone come to my funeral?

You know, important stuff like that.

Well, not so bravely I started up the cliff. At first it wasn't too tough. There were plenty of places to grab onto with my feet and hands. I was halfway up the cliff before I knew it.

"Hey, this isn't bad at all," I said to myself.

Famous last words. Suddenly I looked up and saw nowhere to go. I was stuck.

People started yelling encouraging things from below, like: *Don't panic! You're all right!*

Yeah, right. Easy for you to say. You're not clinging to the side of a cliff 15 to 20 feet above the ground, you bozo! *Whatever you do, don't look down!*

Why not? Is Igor the Sleeping Belayer down there?

Reach up with your right hand! There's a place about two feet above and to the right of your head! You can't see it, but it's there!

Recognizing the voice of my boss, I wracked my brain: "Have I given him any reason to hate me lately?"

Realizing that my strength was draining away fast, and clutching the face of the cliff for dear life, I decided to go for it. I missed. Exhausted and discouraged, I began to have this weird sensation. *I'm going to fall. This is it. I'm never going to see my wife again. I'm never going to have sex again!*

In despair I cried out, "I'm falling!" What else would you say?

And then it was over. There I was dangling in midair off the edge of a cliff . . . completely safe. The ropes had held me up!

I began to enjoy it up there. What a relief! I didn't have to toil and sweat trying to climb up that stupid cliff. I could just hang around and relax. That lasted about 15 seconds, until my boss told me to get back on the mountain and finish the climb.

Oh, yeah, minor details. But I finally made it. After one more "fall" and about five or ten more minutes of exhausting climbing , I dragged myself up over the crest of the cliff and sprawled out in glorious victory. I was at the top!

I had known in my head before I started the climb that the ropes were strong enough to hold me. I also knew that my boss knew what he was doing when it came to rock climbing and that he had secured the ropes properly. But all that great head knowledge turned to craven fear when the moment of truth came and I could hold on no longer.

But then my head knowledge turned to heart knowledge really quick when the ropes came through and saved my life. Then I could relax and enjoy the rest of the climb.

Many Christians go through their lives struggling and straining to make it through. Just the teenage years alone, ages 13-19, can be as draining and exhausting as that rock climb I did. Not to mention the rest of life after that!

But God's Word doesn't say:

> It's all up to you to stand firm in Christ. You're on your own, bud. Sure God forgave you of your sins, but while you're on earth He's saying, "Give it your best shot, my child, and I hope you make it to the top before you fall!"

That's not it at all! Through today's Scripture, God wants you to see how safe and secure you are in Him. He's not only the rope that keeps you safe as you climb; He's also the supernatural energy that gives you the strength to keep on climbing! Go back and read 2 Corinthians 1:21,22 again.

The apostle Peter added his amen to this truth when he wrote:

> Blessed be the God and Father of our Lord Jesus Christ, who according to His great mercy has caused

us to be born again to a living hope through the resurrection of Jesus Christ from the dead, to obtain
an inheritance which is imperishable and undefiled
and will not fade away, reserved in heaven for you,
who are protected by the power of God through
faith for a salvation ready to be revealed in the last
time (1 Peter 1:3-5).

Does this mean God does everything and we do nothing?
No, life is a climb; we have to step out in faith and get on the
cliff and start up. If we never "get in the game," we'll never
experience the exhilaration of making it to the finish line!

Paul put it this way just prior to his graduation to glory
in heaven:

I have fought the good fight, I have finished the
course, I have kept the faith; in the future there is
laid up for me the crown of righteousness, which
the Lord, the righteous Judge, will award to me on
that day; and not only to me, but also to all who have
loved His appearing (2 Timothy 4:7,8).

The Christian life is a fight that needs to be fought. It is
a course that needs to be run. It is a life of faith that needs
to be kept. But God brought you to the starting line and
will be with you to strengthen you and protect you all the
way home. That's a done deal.

So relax and *enjoy* the climb, knowing that His strength
is enough for you. And when things get really tough, you
can *endure* the climb, knowing that the ropes will hold you
up. That's a lifetime guarantee from God Himself.

THE LIE TO REJECT

I reject the lie that I am on my own to live the Christian life and that I have to rely on my own strength, wisdom, wits, and resources to make it.

The Truth to Accept

I accept the truth that God Himself is protecting me to bring me to heaven and that the Spirit within me has been given to grant me the strength I need to make it through life.

Prayer for Today

Dear heavenly Father, I want to thank You for all You have done for me. You enable me to stand firm in Christ. You have anointed me and sealed me as Your own by placing the Holy Spirit within my heart. I thank You that the Spirit is a lifetime guarantee that You will bring me to heaven to enjoy the eternal inheritance that awaits me there. I'm so glad that it is Your power, not mine that protects me through faith as I live life on this hostile planet, behind enemy lines. Give me strength today, I pray, for the fight, the race, and the climb that await me. No matter what, strengthen me to keep the faith. I know it will all be worth it when I receive the crown of righteousness on that future day in heaven. In the name of Jesus, the righteous Judge. Amen.

Read All About It

2 Timothy 4

Going Deeper with God

1 Peter 5

IT'S A SPIRIT THING

If we live by the Spirit, let us also walk by the Spirit (Galatians 5:25).

It wasn't like Brad at all. He was so shocked at his behavior that he called me up on the phone to tell me all about it.

Brad had returned to the Marine base where he lived and worked after I took him through *The Steps to Freedom in Christ.* He had walked into the room a confused, frustrated, defeated Christian. He had walked out feeling "cleaner than he had for years," filled with new hope and a sense that God was giving him a second chance.

"I can't believe what's happened to me," Brad began as I listened over the phone.

"I was working today when all of a sudden I started singing these praise songs. Out loud! I was singing songs that I had learned years ago and didn't even know I had remembered. And I was worshiping God so deeply that I started lifting my hands to the Lord.

"Then I realized where I was and so I stopped, went around the back of the building, and finished my worship service!"

I couldn't help but laugh over the phone as I got this picture of a big, strong Marine worshiping God like that. I was glad for him.

"But that's not all, Rich. Later on, when I sat down to have lunch, I started thanking God for my food. Out loud! I haven't done that for as long as I can remember.

"Then later on in the afternoon something really weird happened. My boss came over and was ragging on me about something and I was about to mouth off at him. But then I stopped. I just kept my mouth shut. Usually I would blurt out something and then feel guilty later for doing it. But this time I kept my cool."

Immediately my mind put one and one and one together and came up with Ephesians 5:18-21. See if you can pick up what I picked up:

> Do not get drunk with wine, for that is dissipation, but be filled with the Spirit, speaking to one another in psalms and hymns and spiritual songs, singing and making melody in your heart to the Lord; always giving thanks for all things in the name of our Lord Jesus Christ to God, even the Father; and be subject to one another in the fear of Christ.

"Brad, do you know what you've just described?"

"What?" he asked excitedly.

"You have just illustrated in the most beautiful way a perfect three-point outline of what happens when you're filled with the Spirit. Brad, you are filled with the Holy Spirit! That's why you're acting the way you are!"

It shouldn't surprise us that when God takes over our lives, things change—dramatically. Hate turns to love.

Bitterness and unforgiveness are replaced by mercy. Faith overcomes fear. And selfishness is swallowed up in service. Not all at once, of course. But slowly, like the ripening of fruit on a vine (check out John 15).

Many Christians live, unfortunately, by the "God helps those who help themselves" philosophy of life. There's just one problem with that saying: It's wrong! It would be much closer to the truth to say, "God helps those who have come to the end of themselves," as Jesus' disciples learned one day:

> He made His disciples get into the boat and go ahead of Him to the other side to Bethsaida, while He Himself was sending the multitude away. And after bidding them farewell, He departed to the mountain to pray. And when it was evening, the boat was in the midst of the sea, and He was alone on the land. And seeing them straining at the oars, for the wind was against them, at about the fourth watch of the night He came to them, walking on the sea; and He intended to pass by them. But when they saw Him walking on the sea, they supposed that it was a ghost, and cried out; for they all saw Him and were frightened. But immediately He spoke with them and said to them, "Take courage; it is I, do not be afraid." And He got into the boat with them, and the wind stopped; and they were greatly astonished (Mark 6:45-51).

What a contrast between a life lived by trust in God and a life of self-effort! Jesus was on the mountain in prayer; the disciples were huffing and puffing at the oars, unable to muster enough strength to row their boat ashore.

Did you notice what Mark said Jesus was going to do? He wrote, "He [Jesus] intended to pass by them." Not stop and get in the boat, but pass by.

Do you think that sounds a little cold and insensitive? After all, hadn't Jesus been the One who had sent them out in the boat in the first place? And weren't the disciples trying their best to make it on their own?

But there you have it: *The disciples were trying to accomplish the will of Jesus on their own strength.* And Jesus was going to walk right on by them. Why? Because they were too busy *trying* that they forgot they were supposed to be *trusting* God.

Count on it: Jesus will always intend to pass by the busy, self-sufficient person. As long as we are straining at the oars, determined in our stubborn self-will to beat the winds that oppose us, Jesus will pass us by.

When was it that Jesus turned toward the boat to help the disciples? When they cried out in fear. Sometimes it takes a real shock in our lives to wake us up and show us we desperately need God.

And when Jesus got in the boat, their fear (of the "ghost") was gone, their straining at the oars ended, and they just stared at Jesus. They knew then that everything was under control. Not *their* control, however—*His* control.

And the wind stopped.

Each of us who "live by the Spirit"—that is, have been born again by the Spirit of God (see John 3:1-12)—have a choice to make: We can walk by the flesh or by the Spirit.

Someone once said, "As Christians, we need to pull in the oars and put up the sails." Translation? Stop trying to row, row, row the boat of your life. Instead, let the wind of the Spirit of God fill your sails.

That sure sounds like sound advice to me!

Let me ask you a personal question: Are *you* filled with the Spirit today? Can you relate to the life which our Marine friend, Brad, was living after his counseling appointment?

Or can you relate more to the tired-out, stressed-out disciples rowing hard but getting nowhere fast?

Remember this: *The Almighty God of the universe calls your body the temple of the Holy Spirit* (1 Corinthians 6:19,20). This means that a power much greater than your own lives in you. He is ready to unleash His strength on your behalf, but He waits for your signal—a cry of distress that says, "I can't row against the wind anymore, God. I need to trust Jesus to get me across."

So go ahead and trust Him to fill you with the Spirit today. If you're a Christian, the Holy Spirit is already *resident* in your life. Why not make Him *president* right now?

The Lie to Reject

I reject the lie that the filling with the Spirit only comes as some great emotional experience or must always be accompanied by unusual, supernatural gifts.

The Truth to Accept

I accept the truth that the filling with the Spirit comes as I choose to trust in God and His resources rather than relying on myself. I welcome any experience God wishes to give me, but refuse any other.

Prayer for Today

Dear heavenly Father, I know that Your Spirit's ministry in my life is to a certain extent a mystery, because Your ways and thoughts are much higher than mine. But I do know that Your Word commands me to be filled with the Spirit. I want to be obedient to You and not walk proudly and stubbornly in my own ways. I have to admit that for much of my day I run kind of on automatic pilot, not giving much thought to You and Your will. I want that to change now. As Romans 12:1,2 says, I choose to present my body to You as a living and holy sacrifice. I want to be transformed by the renewing of my mind and not squeezed into the world's mold. I trust Your Spirit to fill— direct and empower—my life now. In Jesus' name. Amen.

READ ALL ABOUT IT

Galatians 5

GOING DEEPER WITH GOD

Philippians 1

OUT OF THIS WORLD

Peace I leave with you; My peace I give to you; not as the world gives do I give to you. Let not your heart be troubled, nor let it be fearful (John 14:27).

What things would really make you nervous and anxious? How about being called in to meet with your school principal, knowing that he was furious with you? What about standing up in front of a large group of fellow students and telling them clearly about your faith in Christ... right in school! How about both of those things in one day? That's what Jason had to face.

Jason was a senior, just two months away from graduation. He was well-known at the school for playing on the football team, and was generally well-liked. He could easily have coasted his way through the spring of his senior year, graduated, and been out the door and gone while being known as "that nice football player."

But that wasn't good enough for Jason. A student at his high school had recently committed suicide and he knew there had to be others out there who were hurting as well. Jason, being a committed Christian young man, couldn't just stand around and do nothing.

He came to me and asked me what I thought he should do. Knowing the hostile atmosphere toward outspoken Christians at his school, I told Jason that I really didn't know. We decided to pray, asking God what he should do, and a plan began to unfold in Jason's mind. He would go up on the platform in the cafeteria during his lunchtime and share his testimony of what Christ had done for him. Then he would invite anyone who was going through a tough time to come see him afterward.

Jason was pumped. We decided on the date he would do this and rallied all the other Christian students around him to pray. I had never seen such a buzz of excitement as developed over the days preceding this event!

Personally, I was concerned about Jason, knowing that the school administration had tried to intimidate Christians who shared their faith before. But Jason was cool, calm, and collected about the whole thing. "What can they do to me anyway? I'm out of here in a couple of months!" That was his attitude.

Finally the day came. I was on my knees the whole time during Jason's lunch. I was dying of curiosity to know what had happened. I didn't have to wait long.

When he got up to speak, the cafeteria was so noisy that only about a third of the lunchroom could actually hear him. The other two-thirds were pretty clueless about what was happening. Jason asked other Christians in the audience to stand and identify themselves, so that they too could be a resource for hurting students. I imagine that was a real moment of truth for many of the believers in that room, deciding whether to stand up for Jesus or not!

Those who heard Jason speak said he came across very caring and sincere, concerned about the secret struggles of students that can prompt them to commit suicide. He warmly welcomed anyone who was hurting to come and talk with him. Nobody did.

What *did* happen (typical of that school) was that seven angry, "offended" students went running to the administration to complain about Jason's talk. Within an hour or so, Jason was called in to face a furious principal.

Angrily, the man threatened to stop Jason from graduating if he ever tried "a stunt like that again."

When Jason told me the story of all that happened, he was smiling and at peace. I was furious, ready to fly in the sharpest Christian attorney I could find, but Jason knew that he had been obedient and that God would protect him.

I have never seen a more bold stand for Christ by a high school kid. It didn't matter to me (nor to God, by the way) that no one came up to Jason and asked for help. To me that young man is a hero. May the Lord raise up many more like him.

In the early days of the church in Jerusalem, Peter and John had the privilege of seeing a lame man healed outside the temple. He was the one who went "walking and leaping and praising God."

Quickly a crowd gathered to gawk in amazement at what had happened, so the two apostles grabbed the chance to give glory to God. They made sure the people knew that it was the power of Jesus that had healed the man, and they challenged the crowd to repent and turn to Him.

Furious at this latest outbreak of "Jesus freaks," the priest, the captain of the temple, and the Sadducees grabbed Peter and John and threw them in jail, no doubt for "disturbing the peace."

Called before the high priest, Annas, and his nasty group of cohorts, the two apostles were commanded to give an account of what they done. Peter and John were glad to oblige, and Luke was kind enough to record what they said:

> Peter, filled with the Holy Spirit, said to them, "Rulers and elders of the people, if we are on trial today for a benefit done to a sick man, as to how this

man has been made well, let it be known to all of
you, and to all the people of Israel, that by the name
of Jesus Christ, the Nazarene, whom you crucified,
whom God raised from the dead—by this name this
man stands here before you in good health. He is
the stone which was rejected by you, the builders,
but which became the very cornerstone. And there
is salvation in no one else; for there is no other name
under heaven that has been given among men by
which we must be saved" (Acts 4:8-12).

The sermon lasted less than a minute, but cut like a sword
to the very hearts of those who heard it. The sermon was
given before the very men who had conspired to put Jesus
to death and who could have done the same to Peter and
John. It was given with an unearthly boldness and confidence that could not be denied. Look at the reaction of the
Jewish leaders:

Now as they observed the confidence of Peter and
John, and understood that they were uneducated
and untrained men, they were marveling, and began
to recognize them as having been with Jesus (Acts
4:13).

So astounded were they at Peter and John's bold preaching and peaceful confidence that they were reminded of
Jesus. Flustered and frustrated, they could think of nothing
to say, because an undeniable miracle had taken place.

So they tried to pull rank on them and commanded them
not to talk about Jesus anymore. Peter and John's response?
They replied with that same infuriating calmness and boldness:

Whether it is right in the sight of God to give heed
to you rather than to God, you be the judge; for we

cannot stop speaking what we have seen and heard (Acts 4:19).

Not wanting to lose face and appear defeated, the religious leaders threatened the two with further punishment if they did not stop rocking the religious boat. And then they let them go. They had no choice.

Jesus made a promise to us that He would give us His peace. Not a peace like people in the world without Jesus have, a peace that is gone with the wind when tough times come. No, the kind of peace Jesus gives us gets stronger under trial while other people quake with worry and fear.

Don't look for Jesus' kind of peace to come from anywhere or anything in this world, because you'll never find it. Why not? Because it's *out of this world*.

THE LIE TO REJECT

I reject the lie that true peace can be found in anything or anyone that the world has to offer. I refuse to try to calm my worries or fears with drugs, alcohol, sex, eating, food, or any other means apart from Jesus.

THE TRUTH TO ACCEPT

I accept the truth that the peace of God which goes beyond all human understanding will guard my heart and mind in Christ Jesus as I pray and thankfully trust God for His protection and care.

PRAYER FOR TODAY

Dear heavenly Father, I know that the world says that peace comes from not making any waves or rocking the boat. But You have called me to boldly witness for Christ through the power of the Holy Spirit (Acts 1:8). I thank You that when I do so, Your peace will calm my worries and fears and enable me to confidently take a stand for Christ. "When I said, 'My foot is slipping,' your love, O LORD, supported me. When anxiety was great within me, your consolation brought joy to my soul" (Psalm 94:18,19 NIV). I thank You today for the peace of Jesus that does not fade, but grows stronger under fire. In the name of Jesus, the Prince of Peace. Amen.

READ ALL ABOUT IT

Acts 4

GOING DEEPER WITH GOD

Philippians 2

WILL THE REAL JESUS PLEASE STAND UP?

Jesus Christ, the faithful witness, the firstborn of the dead, and the ruler of the kings of the earth (Revelation 1:5).

Muslims say He was a great (but not the greatest) prophet of God. New Agers say He achieved God-consciousness and was one of many "incarnations" of God. Most Jews would say He was a good, moral teacher; some would say He was a heretic.

Liberal scholars have sliced and diced the New Testament to figure out what Jesus said and didn't say, did and didn't do. The so-called "Jesus Seminar" has met twice a year since 1985. They have concluded that only about 18 percent of what the four Gospels record as the words of Jesus were actually said by Him! In fact, they believe that nothing at all in the Gospel of John was actually spoken by Jesus!

Most Americans at Christmastime think of Him as a meek and mild little baby boy. During the rest of the year they rarely think of Him at all.

But C.S. Lewis, skeptic and agnostic turned Christian, presented a powerful argument on Jesus' claims to be God:

> A man who was merely a man and said the sort of things Jesus said wouldn't be a great moral teacher.

He would either be a lunatic—on a level with the man who says he's a poached egg—or else he would be the Devil of Hell. You must make your choice. Either this man was, and is, the Son of God, or else a madman or something worse. You can shut Him up for a fool, you can spit at and kill Him as a demon, or you can fall at His feet and call Him Lord and God. But don't let us come with any patronizing nonsense about His being a great human teacher. He hasn't left that open to us. He didn't intend to.[1]

There is so much confusion in people's minds today over who Jesus really was and is. I can't wait until the real Jesus stands up and shows Himself to all the world. That day may be closer than we think.

While the apostle John was serving his prison sentence (for preaching the gospel) on the lonely island of Patmos, he had an encounter with Jesus that rattled him to the core.

One Sunday he was in prayer when he heard a voice behind him like the sound of a trumpet. Whirling around to see who had mysteriously appeared on that deserted island, he saw the resurrected and glorified Lord. And what he saw scared him to death.

He recorded it for us in Revelation 1:12-16 because God wanted you and me to catch a glimpse of the real Jesus, too. He's not a baby anymore; He's all grown up. He's not one of many great religious leaders; He's the Son of God. And He's not just a wonderful prophet or teacher; He's the King!

I turned to see the voice that was speaking with me. And having turned I saw seven golden lampstands, and in the middle of the lampstands one like a son of man, clothed in a robe reaching to the feet, and girded across His breast with a golden girdle. And His head and His hair were white like white wool,

like snow; and His eyes were like a flame of fire; and
His feet were like burnished bronze, when it has
been caused to glow in a furnace, and His voice was
like the sound of many waters. And in His right
hand He held seven stars; and out of His mouth
came a sharp two-edged sword; and His face was
like the sun shining in its strength.

Not exactly the picture of Jesus most people would
describe if you asked them, is it? It's certainly a far cry from
the skinny, stringy-haired, blue-eyed, fair-skinned guy carrying a lamb that you see in so many religious pictures.

Our Scripture for today describes Him as "the ruler of
the kings of the earth." The President of the United States
may not know it, but Jesus is his boss! The Premier of China
certainly does not know it, but Jesus is his boss, too!

It would be a good idea for them and every other gov-
ernment leader (local, state, national) from every country
to read Isaiah 40:21-25. This is just part of Jesus' job description:

Do you not know? Have you not heard? Has it not
been declared to you from the beginning? Have you
not understood from the foundations of the earth?
It is He who sits above the vault of the earth, and
its inhabitants are like grasshoppers, who stretches
out the heavens like a curtain and spreads them out
like a tent to dwell in. He it is who reduces rulers to
nothing, who makes the judges of the earth meaningless. Scarcely have they been planted, scarcely
have they been sown, scarcely has their stock taken
root in the earth, but He merely blows on them, and
they wither, and the storm carries them away like
stubble. "To whom then will you liken Me that I
should be his equal?" says the Holy One.

Maybe you've been tempted to think that following Jesus isn't worth it. Maybe you've decided it is too hard or too complicated or not worth the hassle of being made fun of by others. Maybe you've thought that you should just forget about following Jesus for awhile, and get involved more deeply in other things—easier things, things everybody else is doing.

Well, think again.

The real Jesus is about to stand up. And when He does, the whole world will bow down. Why? Because He is the King.

You see, Jesus is not just a good moral teacher or a wise prophet. He is the faithful witness, and everything He says is true. He is the firstborn of the dead. He is the ruler of the kings of the earth. He is in charge, and one day He's going to come and personally remind everybody of that fact.

Thinking that it might cost too much to follow Jesus? Think again. Think about how much it will cost *not* to follow Him!

The Lie to Reject

I reject the lie that Jesus is just one of many great religious leaders or moral teachers. I refuse to give in to the devil's deception that it is not worth it to follow Jesus since He is nothing special.

The Truth to Accept

I accept the truth that Jesus is Almighty God and the ruler over all the kings and leaders of earth. I affirm that it is worth it to follow Jesus because He is in charge and will one day fully exercise His authority as King.

PRAYER FOR TODAY

Dear heavenly Father, I thank You for the crystal-clear truth of Your word. While the world around wallows in confusion and doubt over the identity of Jesus, You have left no doubt in Scripture. I worship You, Lord Jesus, for You are the faithful witness and the firstborn of the dead and You rule over all. I praise You that You are the One who raises up one leader and puts down another. And the fact that so many people in this world deny Your Lordship does not change the fact that You are Lord! Today, no matter how tough it is to follow You, I choose to do so, because I know that in the long run it will all be worth it. I wait eagerly for You to come again Lord Jesus. In Your name I pray. Amen.

READ ALL ABOUT IT

Revelation 1

GOING DEEPER WITH GOD

Philippians 3

Day Thirty-Seven

Rock Solid

Jesus Christ is the same yesterday and today, yes and forever (Hebrews 13:8).

Puberty. The mere mention of the word is enough to send chills up the spines of parents of teens...not to mention the teens themselves! Why? Because this time of transition between childhood and adulthood is a period of explosive change.

For many young people, it seems like their body has declared war on itself as powerful hormones blast through the body like a flash flood. A guy's voice begins to change, causing it to "crack" at embarrassing times (like when he's asking a girl out). A girl's body revs up its monthly cycle, a process that will repeat itself 400 to 500 times during her life (minus pregnancies, times of nursing babies, etc.) Isn't that comforting?

This civil war that breaks out on a poor unsuspecting teen or preteen can send his or her moods up and down like a roller coaster. One moment a guy can be all pumped up about his new muscles and the next minute he can be in the pits over a new zit. A girl can get off the phone sky-high after talking with a guy she likes. Seconds later, however, she can turn on her parents like a wildcat when they ask, "Who were you talking to on the phone, dear?"

In my opinion, the two greatest qualities you can have to get you through these wild and crazy teenage years are your faith in God and a sense of humor—especially if you can let your guard down and laugh at yourself once in a while. The following was written to parents of teens, but I hope you're honest enough with yourself to smile, too:

You Know Your Child Is Becoming a Teenager When—

> *You hear the bathroom door close and lock.*
>
> *Your child asks to be dropped off a block away from school.*
>
> *Your child can never find a pen to do homework, but knows exactly where a comb is.*
>
> *Your child can have a clean room in four minutes as long as no one opens the closet door.*
>
> *The refrigerator door is opened more than it's closed.*
>
> *Your child is positive he knows more about everything than you.*
>
> *He or she is sure that you were never a teenager.*
>
> *Your child takes an hour to get dressed to simply walk the dog.*
>
> *Your child's favorite answer is "I dunno," favorite thing to do is "nuthin'," and favorite place to go is "nowhere."*[1]

For some people, the teenage years are the most fun, lighthearted, and exciting days of life. Others (like me!) would not take a million dollars to go through those years again. But for everyone, whether good or bad, easy or hard, joyful or sorrowful, puberty is a time of intense change.

If you're feeling the gusty winds of change hitting you from all sides, continually knocking you off balance in life, take heart! There's a place you can run to, a place of security and stability, a rock that doesn't roll.

"Jesus Christ is the same yesterday and today, yes and forever." That is good news. No, that is *great* news!

Though it's sad when people stay the same and never change, it's not so with Jesus. You wouldn't want Him to change even if He could. Why not? Because Jesus Christ is perfect!

If Jesus changed, that could mean only one of two things: Either He was getting better or getting worse. If He were getting better, that would mean He had been less than perfect before, and therefore less than God. If He were getting worse, then we'd all be in big trouble, because He's in charge!

What a comfort to know that the Jesus we went to bed loving and trusting will be the same in the morning. You don't have to be afraid that Jesus will "get up" on the wrong side of the throne tomorrow morning.

He is not moody. He doesn't have A.D.D. or hypoglycemia. He doesn't have to take tranquilizers to relax. He doesn't have a quick temper. He doesn't have to work out to get stronger, work longer to get richer, or work harder to get smarter. He is always the perfectly holy, just, compassionate, all-powerful, patient, kind, available, all-knowing God that He always was and always will be.

Even the things around us that seem to be so steady and secure—the rising and setting of the sun, the change of seasons, the movement of the stars—will one day cease. God alone remains the same. Earlier in the book of Hebrews the author wrote (quoting from Psalm 102):

> In the beginning, O Lord, you laid the foundations of the earth, and the heavens are the work of your hands. They will perish, but you remain; they will all wear out like a garment. You will roll them up like a robe; like a garment they will be changed.

But you remain the same, and your years will never
end (Hebrews 1:10-12 NIV).

In the midst of His teaching on the great uproar of change
that will occur at the end of the world, Jesus gave us great
hope by saying:

Heaven and earth will pass away, but My words
shall not pass away (Matthew 24:35).

Jesus never once promised that things would be easy in
life. Change is certain, and what is equally certain is that
many times change is painful. Whether Christian or
non-Christian, rich or poor, male or female, black, white,
Hispanic, Native-American, Asian, or whatever, we will all
go through tough times in life.

Jesus alone is the rock on which we stand, and His Word
alone is our anchor in the storm. Listen to these penetrating
words from our Lord:

Everyone who hears these words of Mine and acts
upon them may be compared to a wise man who
built his house upon the rock. And the rains
descended and the floods came and the winds blew
and burst against that house, and yet it did not fall,
for it had been founded upon the rock. And
everyone who hears these words of Mine and does
not act upon them will be like a foolish man who
built his house upon the sand. And the rains
descended and the floods came and the winds blew
and burst against that house, and it fell, and great
was its fall (Matthew 7:24-27).

Heavy words. Powerful words. And not just idle chatter
by Jesus, either. He was warning you and me that *there will
be* violent storms in our lives. Maybe you're going through
one right now.

What was the difference between the two men? Jesus called one man "wise" and the other "foolish." Why? Well, they both built a house. In other words, both men were trying to build a life of safety and security. And both houses were struck by terrible storms. That is, tough times come to all people sometime in life.

But one house stood and the other fell. Why? *The difference was the foundation.* One man built his house on the rock, while the other built his on the sand.

The foundation of sand? Hearing the teaching of Jesus (God's Word), but letting it go in one ear and out the other. The foundation of rock? Listening to Jesus and then putting what He says into practice.

Tragically, it is possible to go to church and youth group, read the Bible, and even faithfully read all 40 of these devotionals and still be in grave danger . . . if you never put into practice the words you hear.

Do you want to build your life on the Solid Rock? Be a "doer" of the Word and not merely a "hearer" (James 1:22).

Jesus is the Solid Rock. A life built on Him *will be* rock solid.

The Lie to Reject

I reject the lie that security comes from building my life on what I think or what my peer group thinks is the way to live. I refuse to believe the lie that anything in this world is a solid rock like Jesus.

The Truth to Accept

I accept the truth that since Jesus alone is both perfect

and never-changing, building my life on Him is the only wise thing to do.

Prayer for Today

Dear Lord, even though things in me and around me are changing rapidly, You are the same. You are the Solid Rock that brings a deeply comforting security and stability to my life. I can be free from worry and fear, because You remain perfect and unchanging. I thank You that as I build my life on hearing and obeying Your teachings, I will be growing in wisdom. And I thank You that the wisdom of a life built on the foundation of Jesus Christ will be able to stand strong when trials blindside me. In Jesus' name. Amen.

Read All About It

Hebrews 13

Going Deeper with God

Philippians 4

THE DAY IS COMING!

The LORD your God is in your midst, a victorious warrior. He will exult over you with joy, He will be quiet in His love, He will rejoice over you with shouts of joy (Zephaniah 3:17).

July 9, 1991. May 8, 1993. January 13, 1995. Those three days most likely mean very little to you, but to me they are in my top five lifetime highlights. The "Play of the Day" for those three dates was the birth of my three children.

Michelle came first. After a 19-hour "labor of love" by my brave but exhausted wife, Michelle emerged from the warm, wet womb into the hot, humid world of Manila, Philippines. It was the most exhilarating moment of my life. I was a daddy!

Just short of 22 months later, Brian came rushing out after only six hours of labor. A boy! A son! Practically every man's dream come true came true for me. I was weeping with gratitude as I cradled that little guy in my arms and told him the day's baseball scores (just kidding!).

Then came Emily. She was a picnic compared to the other two, because my wife, Shirley, had an epidural the third time. Smart move. This lower spinal pain block enables the delivering mom to feel the contractions but not the pain. It's *almost* fun for the mother having a baby this way. Notice I said *almost*.

The emotions I have felt as a dad have been many.

I wanted to soar through the roof that February evening in 1995 when Michelle (age 3 ½) invited Jesus into her heart and He came in and (in her words) "cleaned [her] out like a broom!"

I wanted to take on the whole kingdom of darkness single-handedly when Brian was tormented for a period of time by fears at night. I was furious.

I just sort of melted with love last night when Emily laid her 15-month-old head on my shoulder as I rocked her before bed. I sang "Jesus Loves Me" to her and she tried to sing along with me!

I know in the future there will be moments of beaming pride, gut-wrenching heartache, hilarious laughter, rollicking fun, tender affection, and perhaps even unbearable grief.

But I know one thing for sure: I would die for those kids and I know Shirley would too. It doesn't matter how many times they mess up, I would descend into the pits of hell, so to speak, in a second if that's what it took to save one of them.

If I as a human being, though still quite selfish and protective of my own time, energy, and "freedom," can love my children this intensely, how much more does God love us?

Today's Scripture says our God is a victorious warrior. Jesus defeated the powers of darkness at the cross and personally rescued us. One day His enemies will be made a footstool for His feet (Psalm 110:1). Feast your eyes on this description of Jesus Christ coming to wage and win war against all evil:

> I saw heaven opened; and behold, a white horse, and He who sat upon it is called Faithful and True; and in righteousness He judges and wages war. And His eyes are a flame of fire, and upon His head are many diadems; and He has a name written upon

> Him which no one knows except Himself. And He
> is clothed with a robe dipped in blood; and His name
> is called The Word of God. And the armies which
> are in heaven, clothed in fine linen, white and clean,
> were following Him on white horses. And from His
> mouth comes a sharp sword, so that with it He may
> smite the nations; and He will rule them with a rod
> of iron; and He treads the winepress of the fierce
> wrath of God the Almighty. And on His robe and
> on His thigh He has a name written, "KING OF
> KINGS, AND LORD OF LORDS" (Revelation
> 19:11-16).

Do you ever wonder when those who practice evil will "get theirs"? It starts right here. Do you ever wonder when the devil is going to pay for all his hideous crimes? This is the beginning of the end of Satan.

I once had a T-shirt that said, "The next time the devil reminds you of your past, remind him of his future."

Jesus' disciples were staring up into the sky when He ascended back up into heaven. They must've been hoping Jesus would boomerang His way back to earth immediately. Two angels were sent to earth to keep everyone in the early church from developing a stiff neck. They declared:

> Men of Galilee, why do you stand looking into the
> sky? This Jesus, who has been taken up from you
> into heaven, will come in just the same way as you
> have watched Him go into heaven" (Acts 1:11).

For nearly 20 centuries we have looked forward to that day. Many people have tried to predict the time of Christ's return even though Jesus Himself told His disciples that "it is not for you to know times or epochs which the Father has fixed by His own authority" (Acts 1:7). In other words, it's none of our business *when* He's coming back, but He *is* coming back!

Make no mistake about it: Jesus, the mighty, valiant warrior, will one day come to wage war. I'm sure He must long for that day when He rides out with the mighty armies of heaven to pour out His long-awaited wrath upon evil. I can hardly wait. But I guess we have no choice *but* to wait, and to tell as many people as possible that He's risen and coming again (Acts 1:8).

Until that time, however, you can rest easy in your Father's arms. You can be excited because God "will exult over you with joy." God gets excited when He looks at you! You can be comforted because God "will be quiet in His love." He wants to tenderly hold you and shield you whether you're awake or asleep. And you can be encouraged because He "will rejoice over you with shouts of joy." Like an exuberant daddy cheering his children on in a race, our Father is our biggest fan.

One day we will see Him face-to-face. That day indeed is coming!

THE LIE TO REJECT

I reject the lie that God will simply sit back and watch evil continue to run rampant in the world. I refuse to give in to despair or any feeling of hopelessness as I look at the world around me.

THE TRUTH TO ACCEPT

I accept the truth that the Lord Jesus will come again in bodily form as a mighty warrior and that all His enemies will one day be made a footstool for His feet.

Prayer for Today

Dear heavenly Father, with every second that ticks off the clock, I know that it gets closer to the time of Jesus' return. What a surprise awaits the world when Jesus comes as a mighty warrior to pour out the terrible wrath of Almighty God! I know that it will be a terrifying thing to fall into the hands of the living God. But I thank You that the Lord Jesus Christ also exults over me with joy. He is quiet, gentle and tender in His love. And He rejoices over me with shouts of joy. Lord, to be part of His army that comes to wipe evil off the face of the earth will be a great and high honor. But to see the Lord Jesus face-to-face will be my greatest joy. Until He comes, I ask for the strength to walk in a manner worthy of Him, and I choose to purify myself just as He is pure (1 John 3:3). In Jesus' victorious name I pray. Amen.

Read All About It

Revelation 19

Going Deeper with God

2 Peter 1

The Buck Stops Here

The LORD reigns forever; he has established his throne for judgment. He will judge the world in righteousness; he will govern the peoples with justice (Psalm 9:7,8 NIV).

It was one of the most frustrating days of my life. It all started because of our efforts to present the gospel to the freshman football team at a Midwestern high school.

The football coach was a Christian and had given his okay for a football clinic with the team. Our ministry arranged to bring in a guest speaker who had played college ball and was currently the chaplain of an NFL team. He was more than qualified to speak to ninth-graders.

We were even sensitive to the fact that the event was to be held on the grounds of a public school. The clinic would be totally about football and then there would be a break. After the break, the speaker would talk about the impact that Jesus Christ could have on their lives, both on and off the field. Athletes not interested in hearing his message could freely leave at the break.

The football coach presented the idea for the program to the vice principal and he immediately said no. He wrote, "If this was for football instruction alone, we would approve. But because prayer and reference to God are forbidden in public schools, we deny the request." And he signed his name.

213

"How arrogant," I thought. "This man is clueless as to what the law really says. Prayer and reference to God are *not* forbidden in public schools!" And, by the way, they have *never* been forbidden.

The administration, however, would not change their mind. So we decided to appeal to a higher authority, the school board. We prepared our case, researching the law, and we even brought in a top-notch Christian attorney who specializes in Constitutional law.

Naturally, the newspapers caught wind of the story and began to build it up as the battle of the century. We even made it on the evening news in that city!

Hostile students at the high school took action of their own. They circulated a petition demanding, "Don't turn our school into a Sunday school!" That became the rallying cry at the high school, and many students signed it. I have to admit it was a catchy slogan, though it totally exaggerated what we were trying to do.

The battle lines were drawn. We tried to mobilize the somewhat dull and apathetic local churches for prayer. We got down on our knees and prayed that God's justice would be done and that students would simply have the freedom to hear the gospel. We were excited about what God was going to do.

Several days before the school board meeting, I had wrenched my knee playing racquetball, so I was hobbling around on crutches. But nothing was going to keep me from that meeting.

The room was jam-packed. Nearly 400 parents, students, teachers, church leaders, and churchgoers filled the place, not to mention the newspaper and TV reporters. The air was filled with the kind of tension and excitement that you would find in a courtroom before a big trial begins.

Unfairly, the president of the school board allowed the high school principal unlimited time to speak in the administration's defense. He took 20 minutes to tell of all the bad things our ministry (mentioning me by name) had done. I couldn't believe the lies and half-truths that were coming out of his mouth. But the crowd was buying it.

It was all I could do to restrain myself while my name was being dragged through the mud. I was made to look like some sort of slippery snake who was secretly sneaking religion into this defenseless school.

After the principal's speech everyone else had the chance to make comments—for three minutes maximum! Some ministers from the liberal churches in town gave their hearty "amen" to slamming the doors on our efforts. The audience applauded. I felt nauseous. Things got worse.

It was time for our attorney to speak. "All right," I thought, "now this crowd is going to hear some facts." And he spoke the truth, naming some of the most important court cases that had ruled in our favor. He did a great job considering he had only three minutes. But the crowd laughed at him.

With a great look of relief and joy on his face, the school board president asked if there were anyone else wanting to make a statement. I was ready to blast the entire group. I didn't care what they thought, I was going to give them three minutes of pure Bible preaching. "If we have to go out," I figured, "at least we can go out with a bang!"

But suddenly my mind went completely blank. It was as if the Lord just pulled the plug on my brain and all my wonderful words drained out and were gone. All I could do was sit there helplessly and take it.

When I got home I nearly put my fist through the wall. Why had God let us down? Why didn't He answer our prayers? Why wasn't justice done? To this day I don't have any answers except one: The final verdict is not yet in.

One day God is going to make it right. One day God is going to make all the injustices in the world right.

Every guilty criminal will be brought to justice, and every innocent person who has suffered unfairly will be vindicated. Every abuser who has ruined the life of a child and escaped here on earth will be punished. Every rich man who has oppressed the poor will "weep and wail because of the misery that is coming upon" them (see James 5:1-6 NIV). On the other hand, every act of kindness done in the name of Jesus will be rewarded (Mark 9:41).

Every careless word that shredded another person's dignity will be judged (Matthew 12:36), and every encouraging word that went unnoticed will be noticed at the throne of God's judgment (Matthew 12:37).

The believer in Christ will not be judged for sin, because "there is therefore now no condemnation for those who are in Christ Jesus" (Romans 8:1). Jesus took the full brunt of God's wrath against our sin so that we could be (and are!) forgiven in Him.

The judgment of a Christian is an evaluation of the quality of our work done for Jesus. Rewards (crowns) will be given out in accordance with what we have done with our faith here on earth. The words of Paul the apostle teach this clearly:

> If any man builds upon the foundation [of Jesus Christ] with gold, silver, precious stones, wood, hay, straw, each man's work will become evident; for the day will show it, because it is to be revealed with fire; and the fire itself will test the quality of each man's work. If any man's work which he has built upon it remains, he shall receive a reward. If any

man's work is burned up, he shall suffer loss; but
he himself shall be saved, yet so as through fire
(1 Corinthians 3:12-15).

A believer's *salvation* is not in question. But how much
of his or her life will stand heaven's test of fire? Only that
which is done for Christ—by His power and for His glory—
will remain. The rest will go up in smoke.

I don't know about you, but I don't want to see all my
life's work reduced to a pile of ashes in front of the Lord
Jesus. I want to hear Him say, "Well done, good and faithful
slave; you were faithful in a few things, I will put you in
charge of many things; enter into the joy of your master"
(Matthew 25:23).

There is another judgment coming, however—a judgment for sin. It is a judgment on those who do not bow on
earth to Jesus Christ as Savior and Lord. It is not pleasant
to think about, but it is real. John saw a vision of it and wrote
about it in Revelation 20:11-15:

I saw a great white throne and Him who sat upon
it, from whose presence earth and heaven fled away,
and no place was found for them. And I saw the
dead, the great and the small, standing before the
throne, and books were opened; and another book
was opened, which is the book of life; and the dead
were judged from the things which were written in
the books, according to their deeds. And the sea gave
up the dead which were in it, and death and Hades
gave up the dead which were in them; and they were
judged, every one of them according to their deeds.
And death and Hades were thrown into the lake of
fire. This is the second death, the lake of fire. And if
anyone's name was not found written in the book
of life, he was thrown into the lake of fire.

It is there, at that throne, that Jesus will finally make everything all right. No more excuses. No more blame. No more passing the buck. No more escapes. Everything will be laid bare and exposed before the Judge. And the Judge will act with complete wisdom and justice for all.

No, the court is not yet in session. There is still time for people to repent and turn to Christ. But James says that "the Judge is standing right at the door" (James 5:9). And when He opens the door, that will be it. The buck will stop there.

The Lie to Reject

I reject the lie that since justice is so seldom done on earth, I must therefore take my own revenge and even the score myself. I also refuse to set myself up as anyone else's judge, knowing that the Judge of all will make all things right one day.

The Truth to Accept

I accept the truth that Jesus will one day bring perfect justice, if not on earth, then certainly in heaven. Every injustice that I myself or anyone else has ever suffered will be made right in His own time.

Prayer for Today

Dear heavenly Father, I see in Your Word that we will all stand before the judgment seat of Christ one day (2 Corinthians 5:10). In light of that reality, I want my life to be filled with the gold, silver and precious stones of work done rightly for Your kingdom. Purify my motives so that

I will not do things for my own glory, but for Yours. Knowing that a terrible judgment awaits unbelievers, I want to be your mouthpiece to bring good news to them while there is still time. Please grant me the eyes today to see people as You see them, and the boldness to preach the gospel no matter what the cost. In the name of Jesus, the coming Judge, I pray. Amen.

Read All About It

Revelation 20

Going Deeper with God

2 Peter 2

THE FINAL VICTORY

Each in his own order: Christ the firstfruits, after that those who are Christ's at His coming, then comes the end, when He delivers up the kingdom to the God and Father, when He has abolished all rule and all authority and power. For He must reign until He has put all His enemies under His feet. The last enemy that will be abolished is death (1 Corinthians 15:23-26).

The queen stood many years ago when the first performance of Handel's "Messiah" climaxed with the Hallelujah Chorus. What else could she do? She knew that she was being brought into the presence of the King. And everyone stood with her. And so everyone since that time who has heard the work performed has stood as well.

The words of the chorus are taken right out of the Bible. Soaring upward like an eagle on the wind, the music climbs to a crescendo of praise and worship to Jesus Christ, proclaiming, "Hallelujah! For the Lord God Omnipotent reigneth! And He shall reign forever and ever! Hallelujah!"

At the end of that chorus there is no announcer explaining the words or the music. There is no "postconcert" commentary by the experts, no play by play recap of the performance with replays and slow-motion highlights. There is no need to say anything, because to say anything would cheapen the event. The music speaks for itself.

During these 40 days we have sought to bring you into the presence of the King. We have taken a journey which, we hope and pray, has opened your eyes to catch a glimpse of your God. A glimpse that was not intended to fully satisfy you but to make you hungry for more. Hungry for a lifetime of plunging into His Word and seeking the face of your Father, God, and King.

We are not going to conclude this day's devotional with the usual closing exercises. To do so, I think, would take away from the impact of the words you are about to read ... the words of our final victory in Christ, the Lamb of God who takes away the sins of the world. This time we'll just let the Word of God speak for itself.

May your heart be moved to soar into praise and worship of the King. May your lips shout, "Hallelujah! For the Lord God the Almighty reigns! And He shall reign forever and ever!" You may even be moved to stand.

> I saw a new heaven and a new earth; for the first heaven and the first earth passed away, and there is no longer any sea. And I saw the holy city, new Jerusalem, coming down out of heaven from God, made ready as a bride adorned for her husband. And I heard a loud voice from the throne, saying, "Behold, the tabernacle of God is among men, and He shall dwell among them, and they shall be His people, and God Himself shall be among them, and He shall wipe away every tear from their eyes; and there shall no longer be any death; there shall no longer be any mourning, or crying, or pain; the first things have passed away."

> And He who sits on the throne said, "Behold, I am making all things new." And He said, "Write, for these words are faithful and true." And He said to me, "It is done. I am the Alpha and the Omega, the beginning and the end. I will give to the one who thirsts from the spring of the water of

life without cost. He who overcomes shall inherit these things, and I will be his God and he will be My son" ...

And one of the seven angels who had the seven bowls full of the seven last plagues came and spoke with me, saying, "Come here, I shall show you the bride, the wife of the Lamb." And he carried me away in the Spirit to a great and high mountain, and showed me the holy city, Jerusalem, coming down out of heaven from God, having the glory of God. Her brilliance was like a very costly stone, as a stone of crystal-clear jasper ...

And the twelve gates were twelve pearls; each one of the gates was a single pearl. And the street of the city was pure gold, like transparent glass. And I saw no temple in it, for the Lord God, the Almighty, and the Lamb, are its temple. And the city has no need of the sun or of the moon to shine upon it, for the glory of God has illumined it, and its lamp is the Lamb. And the nations shall walk by its light, and the kings of the earth shall bring their glory into it. And in the daytime (for there shall be no night there), its gates shall never be closed; and they shall bring the glory and the honor of the nations into it; and nothing unclean and no one who practices abomination and lying shall ever come into it, but only those whose names are written in the Lamb's book of life. ...

And he showed me a river of the water of life, clear as crystal, coming from the throne of God and of the Lamb, in the middle of the street. And on either side of the river was the tree of life, bearing twelve kinds of fruit, yielding its fruit every month; and the leaves of the tree were for the healing of the nations. And there shall no longer be any curse; and the throne of God and of the Lamb shall be in it, and His bondservants shall serve Him; and they shall see His face, and His name shall be on their foreheads. And there shall no longer be any night; and they shall not have need of the light of a lamp nor the light of the sun, because the Lord God shall illumine them; and they shall reign forever and ever.

And he said to me, "These words are faithful and true"; and the Lord, the God of the spirits of the prophets, sent His angel to show to His bondservants the things which must shortly take place. "And behold, I am coming quickly. Blessed is he who heeds the words of the prophecy of this book." And I, John, am the one who heard and saw these things. And when I heard and saw, I fell down to worship at the feet of the angel who showed me these things. And he said to me, "Do not do that; I am a fellow servant of yours and of your brethren the prophets and of those who heed the words of this book; worship God . . . "

Behold, I am coming quickly, and My reward is with Me, to render to every man according to what he has done. I am the Alpha and the Omega, the first and the last, the beginning and the end. Blessed are those who wash their robes, that they may have the right to the tree of life, and may enter by the gates into the city. Outside are the dogs and the sorcerers and the immoral persons and the idolaters, and everyone who loves and practices lying.

I, Jesus, have sent My angel to testify to you these things for the churches. I am the root and offspring of David, the bright morning star. And the Spirit and the bride say, "Come." And let the one who hears say, "Come." And let the one who is thirsty come; let the one who wishes take the water of life without cost. . . .

He who testifies to these things says, "Yes, I am coming quickly." Amen. Come, Lord Jesus. The grace of the Lord Jesus be with all. Amen (Revelation 21:1-7, 9-11, 21-27; 22:1-9, 12-17, 20, 21).

Notes

Day 1: All Heaven Broke Loose

1. Paul Eshelman, *The Touch of Jesus* (Orlando, FL: New Life Publications, 1995), p. 16.

2. Ibid., p. 18.

3. Ibid., p. 20.

Day 8: The Way Up Is Down

1. Timothy Beougher and Lyle Dorsett, *Accounts of a Campus Revival* (Wheaton, IL: Harold Shaw Publishers, 1995), pp. 119 ff.

Day 11: When God Plays Hardball

1. Journal entry from Anne Keay. Used by permission.

2. Ibid.

Day 12: Tornado!

1. The Weather Channel, *1993 Tornado Calendar.*

2. Ibid.

Day 13: I Couldn't Get Out of My Seat!

1. Neil Anderson, Dave Park, and Rich Miller, *The Steps to Freedom in Christ—Youth Edition.*

Day 16: Unclean! Unclean!

1. Charles Colson, *The Body* (Dallas, TX: Word Publishing, 1992), p. 307.

2. Ibid.

3. Ibid., p. 308.

Day 19: The God Who Heals

1. Eshelman, *The Touch of Jesus,* p. 127.

2. Ibid., p. 128.

3. Ibid.

4. Ibid.

5. Ibid., p. 129.

6. Ibid.

Day 23: The Devil's Worst Nightmare

1. "Life on a SWAT Team," in *Reader's Digest,* January 1996, pp. 114 ff.

2. Ibid., p. 115.

3. Ibid., p. 116.

4. Ibid.

5. Clinton E. Arnold, *Powers of Darkness* (Downers Grove, IL: InterVarsity Press, 1992), p. 106.

Day 25: The God Who Serves

1. "And God Created PAIN," in *Christianity Today*, January 10, 1994, p. 22.

2. Ibid.

Day 27: You Don't Mess Around with God

1. Colson, *The Body*, p. 382.

Day 36: Will the Real Jesus Please Stand Up?

1. C.S. Lewis, *Mere Christianity*, as cited in William R. Bright, *Teacher's Manual for the Ten Basic Steps Toward Christian Maturity* (San Bernardino, CA: Campus Crusade for Christ International, 1965), pp. 102. ff.

Day 37: Rock Solid

1. Taken from Young Life, *Raising Healthy Teenagers*, a workshop for parents.

Other Books by Neil and Dave

Bondage Breaker, Youth Edition
Bondage Breaker, Youth Edition Study Guide
Stomping Out the Darkness
Stomping Out the Darkness, Study Guide
Busting Free, Youth Curriculum

Freedom in Christ 4 Teens

Devotional Series
Extreme Faith
by Neil T. Anderson and Dave Park
Reality Check
by Neil T. Anderson and Rich Miller
Ultimate Love
by Neil T. Anderson and Dave Park

Other Youth Resources from Freedum in Christ

To My Dear Slimeball
by Rich Miller
Know Him, No Fear
by Rich Miller and Neil Anderson

Freedom in Christ Youth Conferences

Stomping Out the Darkness
For high school and junior high students

Setting Your Youth Free
For adults who serve youth

Purity Under Pressure
For high school and junior high students

For more information about having a
Freedom in Christ youth event in your area, call or write:

Freedom in Christ Youth Ministries
491 E. Lambert Road
La Habra, CA 90631
(310) 691-9128